BIG SUR INN

Courtesy of Deetjen's, Inc.

"*We are shaped and fashioned by what we love.*"
Johann Wolfgang von Goethe

BIG SUR INN

The Deetjen Legacy

Anita Alan

Gibbs Smith, Publisher
Salt Lake City

First Edition
10 09 08 07 06 5 4 3 2 1

Text © 2006 Anita Alan
Photography © 2006

All rights reserved. No part of this book may be reproduced by any means whatsoever without written permission from the publisher, except brief portions quoted for purpose of review.

Published by
Gibbs Smith, Publisher
P.O. Box 667
Layton, Utah 84041

1-800.748.5439 orders
www.gibbs-smith.com

Designed and produced by Linda Herman, Glyph Publishing Arts
Printed and bound in Hong Kong

Library of Congress Cataloging-in-Publication Data

Alan, Anita.
   Big Sur Inn : the Deetjen legacy / Anita Alan. -- 1st ed.
     p. cm.
   ISBN 1-4236-0012-6
   1. Big Sur Inn--History. 2. Vernacular architecture--California--Big Sur. 3. Deetjen, Helmuth, d. 1972. I. Title.
NA7845.B54A43 2006
728'.50979476--dc22

2006012172

With deep love and appreciation
for my son Noel Douglas Walling,
fantasy writer, designer of games, inspiration

and

for Lisa Meckel,
poet, teacher, wise and compassionate friend.

Bixby Creek Bridge, along the southbound road to Big Sur Inn, 1932.
Photo by Lewis Josselyn. Courtesy California Views, Pat Hathaway Collection.

Contents

Foreword — ix

Introduction — x

1 Nature of the Inn — 2

2 The Deetjens — 14

3 Not Breaking the Harmony — 38

4 Room for Inspiration — 60

5 Feeding the Soul — 82

6 Deetjen on His Own — 106

7 Friends of the Inn — 128

8 Keeping the Inn — 146

Acknowledgments — 158

Afterword — 160

Old Coast Road before completion of California Route One. Photo by Lewis Josselyn.
Courtesy California Views, Pat Hathaway Collection.

Foreword

My earliest memories of Big Sur are captured best, I think, in an old sepia-tone postcard I purchased at the Inn back in the early 1960s. A Deetjen dog, Be-Be, lies peacefully in the foreground.

To this day, Deetjen's remains an oasis, a place to sate not only our thirst for food and good company, but a place to restore our spirit as well! Like an old church, she remains open to the faithful who return year after year to commune there.

It continues to be much more than a country inn, but a spiritual haven to those of us who remember Big Sur the way it was, and the way it continues to be—in an old sepia-tone postcard.

Al Jardine
Founding Member of the Beach Boys

Al Jardine and his family have lived a few miles from Deetjen's for 35 years. He raised his four sons—Matt, Adam, and twin sons Robbie and Drew—on the Big Sur coast, where he lives with his wife Mary Ann and the twins. Grammy Award winner, Al Jardine is the author of the children's book *Sloop John B—A Pirate's Tale*.

Introduction

When Deetjen built Big Sur Inn, he shaped forever the lives within its walls. The rough-sawn siding and hand-hewn beams of his vernacular architecture give the Inn its organic integrity. His crafts and the antiques selected by Mrs. Deetjen produce a sense of substance, of tradition. It feels as though the Inn keeps you cushioned from a part of the world that cannot be trusted, but at the same time encourages you to join the world as you wish it could be. The Inn's thin batten-board walls keep your secrets. Its rooms offer a sense of protective dignity, of monastic living—simplicity but with grace and comfort. Nearly everyone who passes through, who stays or lingers, relates to the Inn's intrinsic charm. All who feel the intensity and warmth within these walls will understand the purpose of this book. When multitudes of people say they feel at home here, it is worth taking the time to discover why.

This book contains but a fraction of the flood of memories, my own and those of others, that the Deetjens and their Inn evoke. These vignettes, photographs, and poems remain a loving, uplifting, invigorating part of my life and the lives of untold guests. Few places in the world blend so well with their natural surroundings and offer the visitor such an inviting place to rest, to discover another lifestyle, and to rediscover their sometimes-ignored inner life. Big Sur Inn stands as the extension of two extraordinary lives: the timeless legacy of Helmuth and Helen Deetjen. I write this with deep appreciation for all those who devote themselves to keeping the Inn and its traditions alive.

LOOKING BACK

The book you hold found its way from my hands to yours by both chance and lifelong design. When my old Chevy sputtered to a stop in the driveway south of Castro Canyon and refused all attempts to start, it set events in motion that still connect me with that one moment in time. That night, flashlight in hand, my friends and I made our way from the stalled vehicle up the path toward the light in a window. How could we know the light came from Lower Creek, at that time Big Sur Inn's most distant room? Its welcoming overnight occupant pointed the way across the bridge to the rest of the Inn and—as further chance would have it—the restaurant where I'd enjoyed breakfast just over a year before and hoped to find again. Already a homecoming!

We stayed the night above the Deetjens' room in Top Antique, where one of my friends fell ill and required emergency surgery in Monterey. I stayed with her young daughter at Deetjen's, moving to the Fireplace Room, where we awaited her mother's diagnosis and that of the disabled Chevy. Both recovered nicely, but by the time they had, my first stay at the Inn had lasted an unintended week. That first impression lasted a lifetime. After we had dined each evening with the enigmatic Deetjen at his Family Table, I felt magnetically drawn to the Inn. Mrs. Deetjen was seriously ill and bedridden then, but both she and Mr. Deetjen took to my friend's daughter. While AAA repaired the car, Deetjen arranged transportation for the little girl to visit her sick mother. Helen and Helmuth adored children and welcomed them at the Inn, although I learned they had none of their own.

Whatever sensory impressions I felt during that first stay, they combined to bring me back to Deetjen's time after time. I thought back to a long-remembered family sojourn into the Big

Sur redwoods, and wondered whether, as a child, my family had stopped at the Inn. It felt familiar—the pine scent of the fireplace, the lounging cats and dogs, the inviting antique warmth. The purposeful bustling of the young employees, the summer camp environment that Deetjen's-of-the-Sixties evoked, and the baroque music that cloaked the Inn at breakfast made it feel like home. At least, it kindled in me a symbol of what home should feel like. The stunning infusion of beauty held me gently captive. The simplicity at Deetjen's entreated me to stop and take stock of the world and my place in it from another perspective. The Inn demanded a saner pace than the course I had set. Its European appearance made staying in one place feel like travel. In the quest to find a place that made my heart reach for the heavens, Deetjen's light shone brightest. The Inn became a safe harbor for me, as it did for countless others.

I never worked for Deetjen, though he asked me to year after year. However, when I stayed, I loved being part of the activity of the Inn. I put together five scrapbooks for him: three with durable pages I brought from Japan, one leather-bound book from Spain designed for historic photos, and a birthday scrapbook for Deetjen, black and white, made in Henry Gilpin's advanced photography class at Monterey Peninsula College. "You should be doing this for a living," Deetjen would say, and because he enjoyed them so much, I put together scrapbooks until he died. Most of the vintage photos in this book came from loose pages originally found in those scrapbooks. They remain with Deetjen's, Incorporated, and the Big Sur Inn Preservation Foundation, as does my gratitude for their maintenance. Through the years, the Inn inspired me to take thousands of photographs, many of which I have included here. Additionally, Pat Hathaway of California Views provided photos, technical assistance, and help locating photographers.

Helen Haight Deetjen's scrapbook, the only one that remained intact, has its own amusing saga—another chance occurrence. Deetjen spent a great deal of time viewing that book's pictures and remembering the beginnings of the Inn. He would peer at them closely, perusing each print with the

Canyon Cathedral, a Big Sur pageant of light, shadow, and fog.

magnifier he called his "third eye," an oblong looking glass he kept at hand. Deetjen had not seen these photos in years, probably decades. They must have slipped off the bed, then under it, years before. Their rediscovery rested with the serendipitous birth of eight puppies! Several years after the death of Mrs. Deetjen, one last litter of Big Sur Inn puppies came into the world. The proud mother, Lama, had a reputation for being protective in the extreme and she chose the crawl space under Deetjen's built-in bed as her nest. When time came to find homes for the puppies, I joined the contingent of employees and crawled under for the last pup, but got much more than expected. I felt some paper—not newspaper, I thought. Beneath the fur in the doggie den, almost unrecognizable, was a photo. And another. And another. A later count netted 105 photos. Sandwiched together in stratified layers of

Castro Creek as it flows to sea, 1938.

matted hair, grit, and uncertainty emerged small photographic treasures, protected by Lama and her brood—sepia-toned contact prints of Helen, her family, and her early days of camping in Castro Canyon with Helmuth. With Deetjen's blessing, I took a shoebox full to my tiny darkroom in San Francisco and cleaned and returned them. Then on a later trip, I placed them in the leather album. The earliest picture, taken in 1891, was of Helen Haight as a baby, but the majority of the photos date between 1920 and 1938. Several of them are of Helen, taken by Helmuth when they first came to Big Sur.

The final bit of serendipity regarding this book came in 1969, when I began teaching in Carmel, a life transition from several years of working as a flight attendant. At dinner in Big Sur one Sunday, Deetjen asked if I had found a place to live yet, and I began telling him about the lovely place on San Antonio between 10th and 11th, with a row of cypress trees on both sides of the street. Then he quietly said, "I planted those trees." He then described the house to me in the kind of detail only its builder would know, remarking that it was "up a long driveway."

He even recalled the quarry where he got the stone. However remote the chance, I had the astonishing good fortune to move into one of the two houses Deetjen built when he lived in Carmel and became a caretaker for Mrs. Deetjen, then Helen Haight. Deetjen revisited the little house while I lived there to confirm the location. "This is what I had in mind," he observed.

Without that first Deetjen impression, my life would have taken an entirely different direction. Though the scenery drew me there, it was because of Deetjen and the mystique of his Inn that I stayed and later returned to call Big Sur home for a quarter of the last century. Nor am I alone in that. Many who work at the Inn have stayed for years or returned after quitting. In addition, the Inn attracts a cadre of faithful guests, thankful to see it remain as they remembered.

Deetjen always looked for that child he never had, someone inspired to carry on what he and his wife had established. In a way, he found that in all of us.

Deetjen's own inspiration for coming to Big Sur began in Norway. He read poetry in four languages but favored the English and German poets. Whitman, Emerson, and Jeffers inspired him most among American poets. Here, I must express my appreciation to Jeffers' grandson, Lindsay Jeffers, and all those at Robinson Jeffers Tor House in Carmel, to Stanford University Press and Random House, Inc., for allowing the reprinting of the extraordinary Jeffers poems that begin and end each chapter.

The following Walt Whitman poem was reproduced from the public domain. Though Whitman died the year Deetjen was born, he had a profound impact on Helmuth. The Inn he built fulfilled the promise in a Whitman poem that Deetjen read as a child in Europe. The verse beckoned Deetjen to seek his destiny in California and to settle amidst the redwoods. The poem's setting is on the Mendocino coast, but it mirrors Deetjen's coastal choice of Castro Canyon. Enjoy "these huge precipitous cliffs, this amplitude, these valleys," and view through the eyes of Whitman "the flashing and golden pageant of California."

Song of the Redwood-Trees

Walt Whitman
(1819–1892)

1

A California song,
A prophecy and indirection, a thought impalpable to breathe as air,
A chorus of dryads, fading, departing, or hamadryads departing,
A murmuring, fateful, giant voice, out of the earth and sky,
Voice of a mighty dying tree in the redwood forest dense.

Farewell my brethren,
Farewell O earth and sky, farewell ye neighboring waters,
My time has ended, my term has come.

Along the northern coast,
Just back from the rock-bound shore and the caves,
In the saline air from the sea in the Mendocino country,
With the surge for base and accompaniment low and hoarse,
With crackling blows of axes sounding musically driven by strong arms,
Riven deep by the sharp tongues of the axes, there in the redwood forest dense,
I heard the mighty tree its death-chant chanting.

The choppers heard not, the camp shanties echoed not,
The quick-ear'd teamsters and chain and jack-screw men heard not,
As the wood-spirits came from their haunts of a thousand years to join the refrain,
But in my soul I plainly heard.

Murmuring out of its myriad leaves,
Down from its lofty top rising two hundred feet high,
Out of its stalwart trunk and limbs, out of its foot-thick bark,
That chant of the seasons and time, chant not of the past only but the future.

You untold life of me,
And all you venerable and innocent joys,
Perennial hardy life of me with joys 'mid rain and many a summer sun,
And the white snows and night and the wild winds;
O the great patient rugged joys, my soul's strong joys unreck'd by man,
(For know I bear the soul befitting me, I too have consciousness, identity,
And all the rocks and mountains have, and all the earth,)
Joys of the life befitting me and brothers mine,
Our time, our term has come.

Nor yield we mournfully majestic brothers,
We who have grandly fill'd our time,
With Nature's calm content, with tacit huge delight,
We welcome what we wrought for through the past,
And leave the field for them.

For them predicted long,
For a superber race, they too to grandly fill their time,
For them we abdicate, in them ourselves ye forest kings.'
In them these skies and airs, these mountain peaks, Shasta, Nevadas,
These huge precipitous cliffs, this amplitude, these valleys, far Yosemite,
To be in them absorb'd, assimilated.

Then to a loftier strain,
Still prouder, more ecstatic rose the chant,
As if the heirs, the deities of the West,
Joining with master-tongue bore part.

Not wan from Asia's fetiches,
Nor red from Europe's old dynastic slaughter-house,
(Area of murder-plots of thrones, with scent left yet of wars and scaffolds everywhere,
But come from Nature's long and harmless throes, peacefully builded thence,
These virgin lands, lands of the Western shore,
To the new culminating man, to you, the empire new,
You promis'd long, we pledge, we dedicate.

You occult deep volitions,
You average spiritual manhood, purpose of all, pois'd on yourself, giving not taking law,
You womanhood divine, mistress and source of all, whence life and love and aught that comes from life and love,
You unseen moral essence of all the vast materials of America, age upon age working in death the same as life,)
You that, sometimes known, oftener unknown, really shape and mould the New World, adjusting it to Time and Space,
You hidden national will lying in your abysms, conceal'd but ever alert,
You past and present purposes tenaciously pursued, may-be unconscious of yourselves,
Unswerv'd by all the passing errors, perturbations of the surface;
You vital, universal, deathless germs, beneath all creeds, arts, statutes, literatures,
Here build your homes for good, establish here, these areas entire, lands of the Western shore,
We pledge, we dedicate to you.

For man of you, your characteristic race,
Here may he hardy, sweet, gigantic grow, here tower proportionate to Nature,
Here climb the vast pure spaces unconfined, uncheck'd by wall or roof,
Here laugh with storm or sun, here joy, here patiently inure,
Here heed himself, unfold himself, (not others' formulas heed,) here fill his time,
To duly fall, to aid, unreck'd at last,
To disappear, to serve.
Thus on the northern coast,

In the echo of teamsters' calls and the clinking chains, and the music of choppers' axes,
The falling trunk and limbs, the crash, the muffled shriek, the groan,
Such words combined from the redwood-tree, as of voices ecstatic, ancient and rustling,
The century-lasting, unseen dryads, singing, withdrawing,
All their recesses of forests and mountains leaving,
From the Cascade range to the Wahsatch, or Idaho far, or Utah,
To the deities of the modern henceforth yielding,
The chorus and indications, the vistas of coming humanity, the settlements, features all,
In the Mendocino woods I caught.

2
The flashing and golden pageant of California,
The sudden and gorgeous drama, the sunny and ample lands,
The long and varied stretch from Puget sound to Colorado south,
Lands bathed in sweeter, rarer, healthier air, valleys and mountain cliffs,
The fields of Nature long prepared and fallow, the silent, cyclic chemistry,
The slow and steady ages plodding, the unoccupied surface ripening, the rich ores forming beneath;
At last the New arriving, assuming, taking possession,
A swarming and busy race settling and organizing everywhere,
Ships coming in from the whole round world, and going out to the whole world,
To India and China and Australia and the thousand island paradises of the Pacific,
Populous cities, the latest inventions, the steamers on the rivers, the railroads, with many a thrifty farm, with machinery,
And wool and wheat and the grape, and diggings of yellow gold.

3
But more in you than these, lands of the Western shore,
(These but the means, the implements, the standing-ground,)
I see in you, certain to come, the promise of thousands of years, till now deferr'd,
Promis'd to be fulfill'd, our common kind, the race.

The new society at last, proportionate to Nature,
In man of you, more than your mountain peaks or stalwart trees imperial,
In woman more, far more, than all your gold or vines, or even vital air.

Fresh come, to a new world indeed, yet long prepared,
I see the genius of the modern, child of the real and ideal,
Clearing the ground for broad humanity, the true America, heir of the past so grand,
To build a grander future.

LOOKING AHEAD

Because no one person can speak for the many who love the Inn and think of it as a second home, dozens of people contributed their recollections to this work. If you loved the Inn and left a memento—some words in a journal or your reveries in the embers of a woodstove, or took with you the memory of a candlelit dinner—you had a part in this book. The already lengthy acknowledgments at the end could be a book in itself had I been able to include the multitude of guests, employees, and locals who comprise the character of the Inn. The following chapters and the Robinson Jeffers poetry that frames each one, together with graphics, historical and current photographs, offer a collective impression of Big Sur Inn from the beginning to the present, and hopes for its sustained future.

Chapter One, "Nature of the Inn," re-creates a glimpse of Castro Canyon for the reader, in pictures and description, as the Deetjens first encountered it.

Chapter Two, "The Deetjens," gives the reader background information on the couple who shared the dream of building the Inn, and dared to make it a reality. It contains information and family photos never before published, and hints as to the character of this stalwart, strong-willed pair. Please note that throughout the book, I use the names Grandma and Grandpa, Helen and Helmuth, and Mr. and Mrs. Deetjen interchangeably. Likewise, Big Sur Inn, Deetjen's, and the Inn all refer to the same magical place.

Chapter Three, "Not Breaking the Harmony," reveals the building of the Inn, and shows interior and exterior views of two houses Deetjen built in Carmel in the 1930s. These display the same vernacular architecture he employed at the Inn. It takes you from groundbreaking to the evolution of Deetjen's vision, a condensed version of a Norwegian village nestled gently in this coastal redwood canyon. No need for a ticket or passport for visitors to feel transported to a distant shore!

Chapter Four, "Room for Inspiration," conveys guest's impressions of a stay at Big Sur Inn—through the words left in dozens of journals, and through photographs of the rooms

Big Creek Bridge, traveling northbound to Big Sur Inn, 1937. Photo by Lewis Josselyn. Courtesy California Views, Pat Hathaway Collection.

themselves. The journals represent a cross section of the traveling public, an invitation to share each life, to shock, inspire, commiserate, encourage, and enjoin. These shared feelings offer a unique series of perspectives as couples and individuals, struck by the Old World charm of the Inn, relate their experience from the inside out.

Chapter Five, "Feeding the Soul," invites breakfast and dinner guests to share exquisitely prepared meals, and the musical and antique ambience that make their memory last years beyond the delicious meal. This section features a by-the-glass list of aperitifs, wines, and beers: Additionally, The Inn's chef shares eight coveted recipes. Whether a sunlit breakfast or a candlelight dinner, cuisine at Big Sur Inn brings return visits from locals and worldwide travelers.

Chapter Six, "Deetjen on His Own," covers the time between October 1962, when Helen died, and October 1972, the death of Helmuth—the era when Deetjen entertained and reigned supreme at the Big Sur Inn. It tells about the Inn as so many remember it; before, during, and after Big Sur became household words, and when the nation's nonconformists slipped in name from "bohemian" to "beatnik" to "hippie" in the span of a decade.

Chapter Seven, "Friends of the Inn," is devoted to giving locals, guests, and employees a chance to share memories—tender, biting, poignant, frightening, and funny.

Finally, Chapter Eight, "Keeping the Inn," explores the years following Deetjen's death, the challenges and successes of keeping the Inn operating, the twin foundations that maintain traditions and enhance services at Deetjen's. It shows some "then and now" photos and offers the reader an invitation to contribute to the Inn's future. The task ahead should certainly be an easier one than the Deetjens faced on their own, building in the wilderness during the country's greatest depression and the world war that followed. With love and a spirit of cooperation, the Inn will be here for your great-grandchildren to discover and preserve.

Helmuth Deetjen with dogs, Puppy and Shaggy (pronounced Puppee and Shaggee), 1965, in what is now the Antique Apartment. Photo by Brooke Elgie.

BIG SUR INN

Five Finger Fern along Castro Creek. Photo by Noel Douglas Walling.

one

RETURN

A little too abstract, a little too wise,
It is time for us to kiss the earth again,
It is time to let the leaves rain from the skies,
Let the rich life run to the roots again.
I will go down to the lovely Sur Rivers
And dip my arms in them up to the shoulders.
I will find my accounting where the alder leaf quivers
In the ocean wind over the river boulders.
I will touch things and things and no more thoughts,
That breed like mouthless May-flies darkening the sky,
The insect clouds that blind our passionate hawks
So that they cannot strike, hardly can fly.
Things are the hawk's food and noble is the mountain, Oh noble
Pico Blanco, steep sea-wave of marble.

Nature of the Inn

The magnetic pull that drew Jeffers to the Sur Rivers lured the Deetjens as well. To begin life together in the untamed splendor of this rugged coast remains a choice few make and far fewer sustain. Idyllic Castro Canyon, the Deetjens' chosen refuge and home of Big Sur Inn, covers a cross section of coastal topography, flora, and fauna. Its vegetation ranges from sunny grassland in the upper reaches to dense chaparral on the ocean-facing slopes to the sublime and stately redwoods that brought Deetjen to California. The grove allows enough of the sun's rays to support the lush mosses, ferns, and sorrels that carpet the damp canyon. Like all creeks and rivers of the Santa Lucia Mountain Range and west of the Great Divide, Castro Creek empties into the Pacific Ocean. Though many rivulets drain into it, the creek is not a tributary of any larger stream and flows directly to sea, going through another parcel of land across the highway from the Inn.

The Deetjens chose land protected from the characteristic harsh winds and sometimes sideways-slanting rains along the coastal headlands. They chose well, also avoiding the scorching heat on the hill that overlooks most of their land. That is not to say they sacrificed the chance for a sweeping view of the Pacific Ocean. The upper part of the property has spectacular vistas, and they often picnicked there in the early days of building. Nevertheless, they chose to build their first dwellings in the sheltered place where horses would go during a storm, rather than on the exposed ridge top—a practical decision, as ancillary roads tend to be impassable in the rainy season and building at a higher elevation would have slowed their progress.

FACING: Castro Canyon Waterfall in spring.
ABOVE: Five Finger Ferns, bay leaves, and redwood cones on the bank of Castro Creek. Photo by Noel Douglas Walling.
BELOW: Dew on redwood sorrel.

NATIVE NEIGHBORS

The Deetjens had more than each other and distant neighbors for company. The natural grasses on the upper reaches of their property provided homes for mice, voles, moles, shrews, wood rats, gopher snakes and rattlesnakes, and the much-loved king snakes that stalk and kill rattlers. The skies rendered a canvas for raptors, the red-tailed hawk with its piercing scream, and smaller hawks, Cooper's, and the American kestrel among them. Painted on that majestic backdrop, but less numerous, were golden eagles, peregrine falcons, and other raptors. Evening gave itself over to the sounds of nighthawks, whippoorwills, and owls, the low haunting call of the great horned owl, the higher penetrating cries of the screech owl and several others. Death gives life to nature's solemn undertaker, the good and silent turkey vulture, wheeling, ever-seeking its still prey, the carrion mostly it and insects welcome.

Farther down the slopes in the protection of the chaparral and the forest, they could hear numerous other birds and animals: the whirring wings of coveys of quail, the muted hollow call of mourning doves, the squawks and chatter of Steller's and scrub jays, the staccato hammering of acorn woodpeckers and red-shafted flickers; towhees, crows, kingfishers, water ouzels, blackbirds, sparrows, finches, juncos, chickadees, bush tits, and hummingbirds rounded out nature's orchestra when the Deetjens camped and while they built. The same birds still call, but one needs to listen more intently and in quieter seasons as the highway sounds now compete for attention.

Down along the tranquil stream, the sword ferns, five-fingered ferns, mosses, lichen, fungi, redwood sorrel, and redwood duff create the hushed acoustic soundproofing around the spring surge and the fall trickle of Castro Creek—the first music in the canyon. Under a canopy of towering redwoods, tanbark, alder, coast live oak, and California bay, the riparian corridor sustains more creatures that dodge in and out of grassland, brush, and woodland. The mostly unseen salamanders, newts, frogs, turtles, banana slugs, and the more sporty lizards doing their push-ups in the sun, comprise but some of the sluggish and scurrying motion of the forest understory. The larger animals—deer, foxes, coyotes, mountain lions, and the nocturnal opossums, skunks, and raccoons—round out much of the remaining wildlife seen then as now.

ARBOREAL WONDER

One thinks of a redwood and imagines wide brick-red trunks and skyward-reaching branches, but California has a rarer redwood that attracted both Jeffers and Deetjen. The albino redwood gives the appearance of snow that has fallen on every needle of the conifer but, by some fluke, has missed the ground entirely. If an albino redwood grew anywhere on the Deetjen property, Helmuth kept that to himself. He did say he knew of six white

Foliage from the Albino Redwood that Deetjen brought Jeffers.

redwood locations, but said, "It will take you a long time to find them." Deetjen loved to walk, and as a surveyor he no doubt noted these wonders as landmarks.

The albino redwood, an arboreal anomaly, has the genetic inability to produce sufficient chlorophyll to grow independently. Microscopic spots of green sparsely dot each needle, contrary to the notion that the albino is entirely white. Some albino redwoods reportedly grow to a height of twenty feet. Most however appear as a brush-like growth at the base of other redwoods, and all need nutrients from the parent tree. The albino redwood pictured here grows, carefully guarded, at Fernwood Campground. One gains nothing by picking a piece to take along, for they decay quickly. Once dry, albinos appear the same as other redwood sprigs. Before botanists studied the phenomenon, most people surmised the albinism resulted from a lightning strike. In 1938, Jeffers wrote: "We came down to the Sur River, and passed the albino redwood that still grows there, shining in the forest darkness, shoots of snow-white foliage growing from the stump of a lightning-struck tree: not a human story, but strange enough to be."

Though Jeffers never wrote a poem about the albino, it was a source of fascination for him, and he spoke of it to Deetjen as Helmuth and Helen left Carmel Point to live in Big Sur. In his long-distance walking days, Deetjen would bring a "spray of white redwood" to former neighbor Jeffers at Christmas. He described the trek to town as a pilgrimage.

In a December 1915 letter to Dr. Lyman Stookey, Jeffers wrote of the tree for the first time:

> Last week we drove by mail stage some forty miles south of Carmel—"down the coast," they say here—into the valley of the Big Sur River. A mile or so this side of our destination the stage-driver pointed out what is called the "white redwood"—a quantity of bushy redwood growth, pure albino, around the stump of a big tree. I am enclosing a sprig of the albino (with one of the normal for control), thinking you may be interested. Albinism seems very unnatural in plants, since their life depends on chlorophyll. All the saplings of this stump have white needles; there are no other albinoes, so far as anyone knows, in the forest. It is not caused by lack of sunlight; for the other redwood saplings growing in much denser shadow, are quite normal. The stage-driver's theory is that the parent-tree was struck by lightning, and that turned white the foliage of the root sprouts:—I suppose on the principle of a man's hair turning white with terror!

The letter ended, "The albino is turning a little brown, I see. It was pure white when fresh, like new ivory." Jeffers once described the pines in Carmel as being pygmies compared with redwoods. In size, the albino redwood is closer to the brush that covers much of Big Sur's hillsides, protecting them from erosion.

LOCAL COLOR

To appreciate the coastal chaparral environment to its fullest requires the visitor to observe it in all seasons. The showy wildflowers of spring, summer, and early autumn give way to reseeding and new sprouts. The sun's heat cracks open the ceanothus seedpods, causing them to make tiny spitting sounds as they cast themselves into fertile ground and roads alike. Spring's firmament of wildflowers, manzanita, chamise, coyote brush, locoweed, bush and sky lupine, poppies, lizard tail, sticky monkey—all these fade but unobtrusively prepare for next year's splendor. Birds and small rodents await thimbleberry, coffeeberry, and the bright toyon berry (Christmas berry, California holly) as supplemental food sources in fall and winter.

Fall color here mainly consists of the yellow sycamore trees. Their puzzle-piece beige-barked trunks and branches spread in gnarled stark contrast against the evergreens.

ABOVE: Poison oak in spring.
FACING: Castro Canyon redwoods in fog.

Poison oak leaves generally turn crimson after the first cold spell in autumn. Since the evergreens outnumber deciduous trees, Big Sur's fall colors enjoy a shorter season and more subtle display than experienced East Coast leaf peepers would expect.

But fall does bring a flurry of brilliant orange. Colorful monarch butterflies, which come to overwinter in the Andrew Molera State Park and Pfeiffer Beach areas, arrive from the north about October. By then, at least one rain has usually washed the summer coating of dust from the leaves that border dirt roads. Hints of that rain may come with the sweeping south wind, but a surprisingly good predictor of autumn's first precipitation is the sighting of a tarantula on the road, as amorous males seek the nest of a female. These unfortunate behemoth male arachnids face certain death from exposure or attack once their mating quest begins. They never return to their underground home after their brief stint as mate (and prognosticator). Rain usually comes about ten days after the sighting.

Just a month later, Big Sur experiences its annual southbound gray whale migration. The often-inclement weather that time of year gives the land and the locals a time to regenerate, but promises strenuous activity for road crews. Mudslides and rockslides can happen any time of year, but in winter, they are inevitable on California's Route One.

The mushroom smell of moist earth and leaves after the first autumn rain makes for lovely walks, but any time of year a walk in Big Sur brings sensory delight. The rich mix of black sage and California sage, wood mint, and the more delicate yerba buena merge with salt sea breezes and a variety of other plant life to energize every breath. Though set back from the sea, the haven where the Deetjens chose to build their home and their inn frequently becomes enshrouded in fog, making an even more pungent mixture of scents. Sound as well as smell travels in the mist and amplifies the call of gulls and the bark of sea lions from the rocky shore some distance away.

Starting with such splendor, how does anyone create a sanctuary for people commensurate with nature's purity and solemnity? The Deetjens undertook the impossible. They set about building a place as unforgettable as its surroundings, a place of spiritual and physical renewal. This they did with little but resourcefulness and love.

Sword fern against bark. Photo by Noel Douglas Walling

JUAN HIGERA CREEK

Neither your face, Higera, nor your deeds
Are known to me; and death these many years
Retains you, under grass or forest-mould.
Only a rivulet bears your name: it runs
Deep-hidden in undeciduous redwood shade
And trunks by age made holy, streaming down
A valley of the Santa Lucian hills.
There have I stopped, and though the unclouded sun
Flew high in loftiest heaven, no dapple of light
Flecked the large trunks below the leaves intense,
Nor flickered on your creek: murmuring it sought
The River of the South, which oceanward
Would sweep it down. I drank sweet water there,
And blessed your immortality. Not bronze,
Higera, nor yet marble cool the thirst;
Let bronze and marble of the rich and proud
Secure the names; your monument will last
Longer, of living water forest-pure.

Moss-coated riparian stone.

Carmel Point, Tor House in center, Deetjen and Helen Haight house not yet built—c1930. Courtesy of California Views, Pat Hathaway Collection.

two

CARMEL POINT

The extraordinary patience of things!
This beautiful place defaced with a crop of suburban houses—
How beautiful when we first beheld it,
Unbroken field of poppy and lupin walled with clean cliffs;
No intrusion but two or three horses pasturing,
Or a few milch cows rubbing their flanks on the outcrop rock-heads—
Now the spoiler has come: does it care?
Not faintly. It has all time. It knows the people are a tide
That swells and in time will ebb, and all
Their works dissolve. Meanwhile the image of the pristine beauty
Lives in the very grain of the granite,
Safe as the endless ocean that climbs our cliff.—As for us:
We must uncenter our minds from ourselves;
We must unhumanize our views a little, and become confident
As the rock and ocean that we were made from.

The Deetjens

Helen and Helmuth Deetjens' journey began on distant shores, in different cultures, and with dissimilar backgrounds. However, their common goals and dreams more than made up for those differences. Together they weathered the Depression, World War II, and Cold War eras. Mrs. Deetjen knew the coast with its Bohemians, saw the start of the Beatnik Generation and the Hippie influx. She died in 1962 without seeing some of the greatest changes in Big Sur life, leaving Helmuth to encounter them alone, for the most part, sometimes gracefully, sometimes not.

Public records tell some of the Deetjen story; local residents, former employees, and guests tell more; but campsite photos, so nearly lost, show the truly humble beginnings of the Inn. As the Deetjens took on what would become their life's work, they lived in integrated solitude, each self-sufficient and fiercely independent. To stay long on this coast and in these mountains required resourcefulness and determination. The Deetjens had a limitless supply of both.

Sheer luck filled some of the gaps in Helen's history; for example, finding her family photos while helping employees remove a litter of puppies from beneath Deetjen's bed, several years after Helen's death. Other than that, almost no pictorial history of her exists. Conversely, Helmuth's written family history dates to 1258, more than 500 years before America was even a country! The difficulty with writing Helen's heritage came in finding material; the problem with Helmuth's lay in deciding what to eliminate.

Finding *his* history involved another lucky break. Early in the 1960s, Deetjen received *Die Bremer Familie Deetjen: 1258–1908* with delight, a beautifully bound book of his family's history. In the unsettling early transition period that followed his death, some-

FACING: Helen's open-air kitchen.
ABOVE, TOP: The Deetjens' humble beginnings: camping out near Castro Creek.
ABOVE: The Deetjen Family History Book, *Bremer Familie Deetjen: 1258–1908*, was rediscovered in an auction by longtime Deetjen's chef, Bill De Groat.

one sold the Deetjen volume at auction. But for the attentive eye of Bill De Groat, the chef who held the longest employment tenure at the Inn, the historical account would have ended up on some unknown collector's shelf or, worse, discarded. Though he no longer worked at the Inn, De Groat instantly recognized the volume at a live auction, bid on and bought it, and then returned it to Deetjen's. Without that rediscovery, information on Deetjen would remain scant.

It turns out that the Deetjen family members from Bergen, Norway, and Bremen, Germany, compiled the written and pictorial history of 138 Deetjen families by mail, and never met in person! Written in German, Deetjen's father's native language, the history covered his mother's Norwegian heritage as well. Blank pages inserted at the end of the volume were intended for the use of generations to come, but the pages remained blank, as the Deetjens did not have children of their own. Instead, they built another kind of family heritage, one that welcomed the world into their home, and still does.

HELEN HAIGHT

Georgia-born Helen Haight settled on the Central Coast in the early 1920s. She was born October 22, 1889, but her city of birth was not registered, as Georgia law did not require birth certificates until 1919. In 1900, at age 11, Helen lived in Los Angeles with her mother, Ida, and two half-brothers, Alfred (born 1882) and George (born 1884), sons of Alfred Boyd of Georgia, Ida's first husband.

The 1910 census shows Helen living with her parents, Ida and Will Haight. Her father was listed as District Attorney for the City of Los Angeles. This was the second marriage for Helen's widowed mother. We don't know what happened to Will Haight, only that no further record of him appears, and it's presumed she may have been widowed a second time, as the name Ida Frisbee appears on records as well.

The 1920 records show Helen single at age 29, living on Howe Street in Oakland, California, with her mother and one brother, and employed as a governess for a private family. Helen's scrapbook shows a small, unclear photo of her with her brother Alfred Boyd Jr. and a woman Helmuth Deetjen identified as Mother Pomona, believed to be the head nurse where Helen graduated from nursing school. The 1920 census actually enumerates Helen twice in the Bay Area in separate reports; the second residency was on Presidio Avenue in San Francisco, where she again became a governess, this time for the Haas family. The two Haas-family maids came from Denmark and Sweden and likely shared their Scandinavian customs with Helen, who some years later met and married the Norwegian-born Helmuth Deetjen.

As she came into her own, the independent Helen, a voracious reader and sometimes journal writer, moved to California's Central Coast, an area abundant with both famous and

Helen Haight at age 3 in Georgia.

rising writers and artists, one of the most prominent being her neighbor Robinson Jeffers on Carmel Point. By 1930, she moved from Ocean Avenue in Carmel to Bay View Avenue on Carmel Point, where the Yates family employed her as a medical nurse, likely for Charles Yates, then 69 years old. His wife Eleanor, ten years younger, worked as a retail merchant in a women's apparel shop. Unfortunately, a city employee destroyed the Carmel business records from the years 1916 to 1956, so information on that shop and many others remains a mystery; however, a sign from The Cinderella Shop in Carmel sat outside the Deetjen's room for many years, and some surmised Helen herself once worked there.

For years people believed Helen was related to former California Governor Henry Haight, but no one substantiated the connection between them. Governor Haight was also a banker and philanthropist, and remains the one most often listed as the man for whom San Francisco officials named Haight Street. However, in the early 1850s, four prominent related Haights could make that claim. Three of these pioneers were brothers: Samuel, who was in Stevenson's Regiment in 1847; Henry, a bank manager; and Fletcher, a lawyer and judge. It was Fletcher's son, Henry Huntley Haight, an attorney appointed to a judicial post by President Abraham Lincoln, who later became a California governor (1867–71). One might expect the governor to be related to Will Haight, who was an attorney in the same era and reportedly served as District Attorney for Los Angeles City, but no known genealogical records indicated a relationship. However, Henry Benson, a Big

ABOVE: Helen Haight at 13 in Los Angeles.
ABOVE, TOP: Helen's mother, Ida Boyd Haight.

Helen's father, Will Haight, reading the *Los Angeles Times*.

Sur resident for years and a distant cousin of Helen Haight, frequently visited the Deetjens with his parents as a child. Benson provided the first-hand information from recollection and his family's records that Helen was the granddaughter of Henry Huntley "Happy" Haight, the California Governor.

While Helen lived on Ocean Avenue, she resided near renowned Dutch photographer Johan Hagemeyer as well as architect Samuel Bixby, who would likely have encouraged her interest in the South Coast he so loved. World-famed Bixby Creek Bridge, first named Rainbow Bridge for the rainbow trout far beneath it, now bears Bixby's name. Talk of Big Sur would have appealed to Helen's adventurous spirit and strong will. Those traits, coupled with a love of literature, art, music, and her comfort with Scandinavian culture, were all attributes her Norwegian match, Helmuth Deetjen, would find irresistible. Deetjen's reputation and skill as a builder led Helen to hire him as a handyman and caretaker. He built at least two unique homes in Carmel, and possibly a third, around the time they met. One he constructed on San Antonio, and the other with Helen on Bay View Avenue.

The two Carmelites soon found they shared a common interest in Big Sur—and each other. In time, they chose Castro Canyon as their favorite campsite. Perhaps because of Helmuth's citizenship status, perhaps because of her unmarried status, Helen originally took possession of the 3.95 acres as her sole property, which would house the Inn eventually. The couple would not tie the knot until 1938. The marriage granted Deetjen permanent status in his adopted country and assured Helen the realization of her dream, a home on the land she had purchased.

The purchase of land from Rojelio and Bertha Castro on August 22, 1936, set dreams in motion for both Helen and Helmuth. The same day, Deetjen's good friend and soon-to-be neighbor, sculptor Gordon Newell, purchased adjoining acreage from the Castros. Newell and Deetjen had also camped at Castro Canyon and knew each other before they met their wives. Although moving there was a dream for both of couples, Newell used his purchase only as a vacation home. The price? $1,975.00. The Deetjens paid one quarter

STATE OF CALIFORNIA
CERTIFICATION OF VITAL RECORD
COUNTY OF MONTEREY
SALINAS, CALIFORNIA
MARRIAGE LICENSE
State of California,
State of California,
CERTIFIED COPY OF VITAL RECORDS
JUN 17 2005

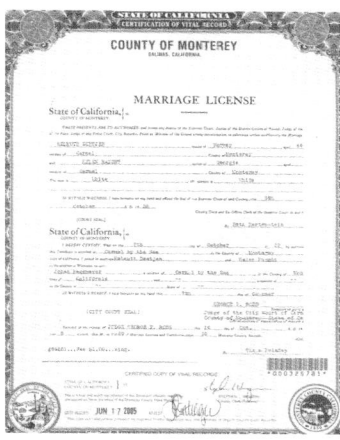

ABOVE: Deetjen-Haight marriage license Certificate.

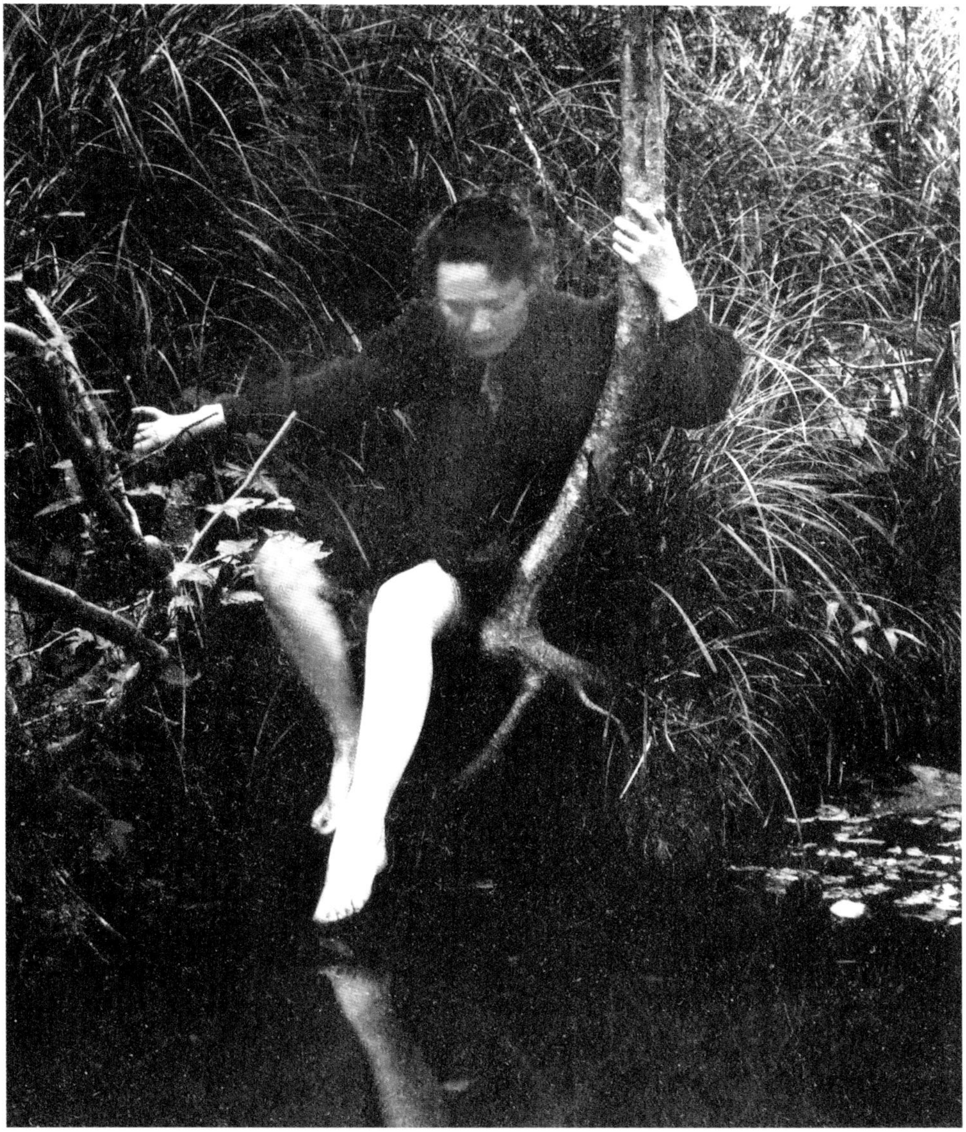

LEFT: Helen takes time to enjoy Castro Creek's chilly waters.

down and three equal payments, the last scheduled for August 22, 1939. Finding such funds during the Great Depression, especially in isolated Big Sur, was difficult indeed, but Helmuth was resourceful and Helen frugal. Records show they made every payment with time to spare.

HELMUTH DEETJEN

When Helmuth Deetjen stepped onto the steamship *Bergensfjord*, April 16, 1924, bound for New York, he changed many more lives than merely his own. He may have signed on as an "Ordinary Able Seaman," but he was anything but ordinary. By then, he had traveled through Europe and to North Africa, and had studied at the university level in Heidelberg and Paris. However, Deetjen remained largely self-educated.

Though a student of literature, metaphysics, art, music, and engineering, people mainly remember Deetjen as a keen observer of nature and human nature, and for the craftsmanship—especially with woodworking and wrought iron—that became his passion. Deetjen needed to find a way to employ his talents and at the same time sustain his philosophical vision. He brought with him every skill and dream he would need for success in America. We know nothing of the other two *Bergensfjord* crewmembers, Severin Stenersen and Oscar Bengtsen, but Deetjen went on to make his mark.

Born in Bergen, Hordaland County, Norway, on November 14, 1892, Deetjen was the

Helmuth Deetjen helped crew the *Bergensfjord* to New York in April 1924. Courtesy of Ellis Island and Statue of Liberty Foundation.

The Deetjen children (photo taken in 1908), from left: Marie (1888), Helmuth (1892), Fritz (1894), Tina (1889), and Otto (1890).

fourth child of five. He had two older sisters, Marie and Tina, an older brother, Otto, and a younger brother, Fritz. His father, Peter Deetjen, was born in Bremen, Germany. Peter's father, Christian Deetjen, established a successful tobacco trade, The Brothers Deetjen, which evolved into two companies: J. C. Deetjen & Co. and Herman Deetjen & Co. A Deetjen-owned firm existed under another name until 1976.

Christian Deetjen married Marie Wolf, a cherub-faced girl who still looked angelic at 75, but what started as a life filled with promise ended in hardship and heartbreak for the couple and their five children. Christian enjoyed great popularity, and became president of the Chamber of Commerce in Bremen, a prestigious appointment. However, Christian died suddenly of appendicitis at age 42, leaving the family heartbroken. Marie hadn't enough money to raise the children, so Peter Deetjen, the eldest, and his two brothers and two sisters had to leave their distraught mother and live with various relatives. At least one child, possibly two, moved to Galveston, Texas, an area with a large German-emigrant population. Peter's mother never remarried but did finally establish a linen store with her sister-in-law.

The Deetjens 23

Oil painting of family escapade hangs in Bremen Historical Museum.

An interesting footnote in all this tells that Peter's maternal grandfather, a war veteran from 1815, was on his way to Russia with Napoleon's army; understanding well the difficulty of northern survival, he and a friend decided to desert and join a hunting club, the Boeseschen Jaeger. An oil painting of their escapade hangs in the Bremen Historical Museum. But for the decision to desert, Peter Deetjen and, of course, his son Helmuth Deetjen would not likely have been born, as that infamous campaign—a narrow, costly victory with enormous casualties—ensured Napoleon's downfall.

In time, Peter Deetjen became deacon of St. Petri Cathedral Church in Bremen, and according to established tradition, the church placed the Deetjen coat of arms in the corridor of the Bremen Boys Orphanage in 1877. Ultimately Peter immigrated to Norway, married Norwegian-born Clara Fleischer, and became a successful tobacco merchant in a Bergen partnership with J. W. Nolte and Son, whose business name Peter Deetjen retained even after he assumed full ownership of the company, thus following the tobacco trade path his father, Christian, had taken in Bremen.

Peter, a skilled woodworker, built the palatial Deetjen estate in Bergen in 1900, where Helmuth Deetjen spent much of his youth. The precocious Helmuth, home-schooled from age 12, would observe and work alongside his father, a 33rd Degree Mason, for a number of years at an impressionable age, thus becoming an apprentice in several trades.

Deetjen's boyhood home still stands in the City Center next to Nygaardsparken, Bergen's largest park, part of the University of Bergen, situated in a mix of private homes and hotels, and now used for student housing. Where the Deetjens lived before the completion of their new home is uncertain, but it might have been near Troldhaugen, Grieg's home, as Deetjen frequently referred to hearing Grieg play piano when he was a young boy. Casting aside the comfort and security of familiar European family traditions that dated back to 1258 could not have been an easy decision for Deetjen. However, at the age of 31, and still unmarried, he chose to leave his homeland to begin his own traditions.

When he docked at Ellis Island after his ten-day working voyage, he set out to see all he could of his adopted country, starting with New York. As a surveyor, builder, and engaging conversationalist, he landed jobs easily. He worked for a time as a surveyor in New York State and Key West, Florida. It remains uncertain whether Deetjen took part in the beginnings of the Tampa, Florida, Rosicrucian Order in 1925, but it's a virtual certainty that he knew of it. That was a small but widening circle in which he moved. He went to Chicago as well, perhaps on a philosophical search, but did not remain long. He continued on to Hollywood, California.

Though studio portraits show him to be photogenic, he actually came to Hollywood less with an interest in acting and more on a spiritual quest. The Rosicrucian Order, Vedanta Society, and Self Realization Fellowship were but a few of the spiritual organizations in Southern California that had strong followings in Hollywood and the Los Angeles

ABOVE, TOP: Oil Painting of Peter Deetjen (born 1856) by Charles Pundsack. Courtesy of John Atkinson.
ABOVE: Oil Painting of Clara Fleischer Deetjen (born 1856) by Charles Pundsack. Courtesy of John Atkinson.
LEFT: Family estate that Peter Deetjen built in Bergen, Norway. Of the two distant figures, Deetjen is on the left.

ABOVE: Deetjen's family home, now part of the University of Bergen, in the City Center. Photo by Cato Kolaas.
BELOW: Deetjen's sheet music from his countryman Edvard Grieg, once a neighbor.

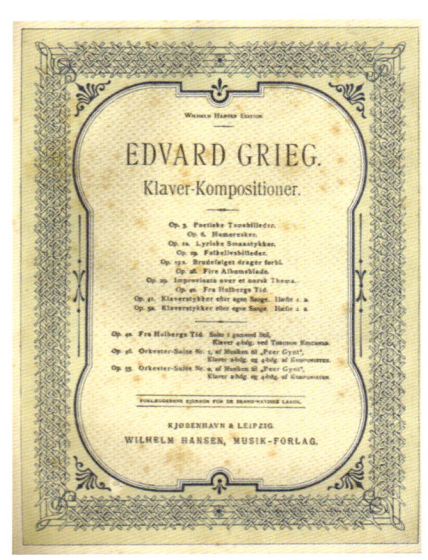

area, and Deetjen's intense interest in metaphysics and various world religions led him there as part of a deeper lifelong search; but the extent of his involvement in any one organization is unknown. The Theosophical Society held its Jubilee Congress in 1925, when Jiddu Krishnamurti was still active. Krishnamurti, who would later visit Deetjen when he was working on the Inn, was also in the Los Angeles area during that time. Deetjen said a Hollywood studio offered Krishnamurti a contract—to play Buddha!

No doubt Deetjen missed the intellectual companionship he enjoyed in Norway, where he had been a great friend of Stein Bugge, and had formed a bond with other painters and writers within the artistic, theatrical, and philosophic circle of Einar Lexow, author and art historian.

In his self-styled college years, Deetjen attended both the University of Heidelberg and Paris. He not only walked across Europe but also met with the famous, such as Rudolph Steiner, who would later found the Waldorf Schools, and the infamous, Adolf Hitler among them. Post War and prewar Europe became a haven to a mix of personalities involved in the arts, philosophy, and political activism on both right and left between 1921 and 1923 when Deetjen spent time on the Continent. According to Bob DeFord, seven-year Inn employee, Deetjen's last words to Hitler were, "You just don't understand the American cowboy," an observation the rest of the world would discover about 20 years later.

In an interview for a Norwegian publication, Norwegian acquaintance Harry Iverson related what Deetjen told him: "He was interested in everything from Nietzsche to the practice of yoga, so the choice stood between India and—Hollywood!" In a somewhat ambiguous translation, Iverson writes, "In the neighborhood of the 'world's dream factory' [a Norwegian-English translation, and Deetjen's wry description of Hollywood], a fabulous spiritual sect had developed," one that promoted world salvation through forms of religion. "This pursuit had been for Helmuth Deetjen, a calling since his early youth," Iverson wrote.

By the early 1930s, but possibly the late 1920s, Deetjen made his way north toward his first view of the redwood trees, the primary inspiration that brought him to the United States and to a life vastly different from continental Europe. Deetjen had seen Europe between wars, and sensed, even predicted, another war would follow World War I. This concern, coupled with the grim vision of postwar Europe, influenced his decision to leave his native country. In Norway, however, he left behind a life that was exceedingly comfortable if not privileged to pursue his own dream, and as the Whitman poem promised, "to build a grander future."

Years into that future, at the 25th anniversary of Big Sur Inn, Deetjen recalled his first encounter in Carmel as he sought employment: "I went up to the newspaper office in Carmel, *The Carmel Pine Cone*, and had a talk with the editor, Perry Newberry. I was a total stranger to him, but I told him exactly the way I stood. And indeed, Newberry turned out to be a real friend. He put his hand in his pocket and gave me all the money he had, $25.00."

Deetjen was so grateful for this extraordinarily friendly gesture that he insisted Newberry suggest a way for him to return the favor. Newberry then told him that he had an unbelievable amount of outstanding bills that maybe Deetjen could help him collect. Deetjen smiled. "Whether you believe it or not," he recalled, "I collected about $3,000 in unpaid bills." In the Norwegian-translated interview, Deetjen continued, "I used neither pressure nor harsh words. I simply made the rounds and told people how kind, generous and understanding Mr. Newberry was, and they all paid."

Not long after the meeting with Newberry, Helmuth Deetjen met Helen Haight. Within a few years, the headstrong couple married in Carmel, he at the age of 46 and she at 48, a first marriage for both. Photographer and friend Johan Hagemeyer witnessed the union, but if photos of the ceremony exist, no one has identified or published them. With thousands of Hagemeyer prints and negatives at Berkeley's Bancroft Library, if there, they may remain unidentified.

Though Helen kept a diary, sadly it was lost, and Helmuth never wrote of their first venture along the Big Sur Coast, unless it was to a Norwegian relative or friend. For many years, he corresponded with his older sister Marie, but no letters from her remain, though an empty envelope *does*. He did, however, paint landscapes and seascapes for pleasure,

ABOVE: Deetjen with the Rosicrucians in Hollywood, c. 1928.
BELOW: Medallion for art historian and author Einer Lexow, Deetjen's friend in Norway.

The Deetjens 27

Deetjen lived in Hollywood, pursuing his interest in metaphysics and the theater, before coming to Carmel.

and on-site house plans for practicality. He joked to friend Joe McLellan that a storm came and all his "watercolors washed away."

Venturing from the west coast of Norway to the west coast of America, Deetjen must have been struck by similarities—steep mountains, streams and rivers, lush plant and animal life, wildflowers, rock outcroppings, and the ocean. The seacoast activities as well, thriving fishing, whaling, and logging industries, no doubt made him feel at home. The differences? No fjords. No aurora borealis. And no snow. In Big Sur, snow is cause for celebration. Though it periodically dusts the crest of the Santa Lucias, one sees snow along the coast only about once a decade, if that. Better weather meant Deetjen could work outdoors almost year round, something he loved. He shared a powerful work ethic with another of his poet mentors, Rainer Maria Rilke. Renowned sculptor Loet Vanderveen recalled, "It's amazing that he built that [Inn] practically all by himself." In a filmed interview for *Big Sur: The Way It Was*, cinematographer Robert Blaisdell recorded Deetjen saying, "You have to have plenty to do if you want to live here, otherwise you go nuts."

Sculptor Jim Hunolt recalled,

He was always asking me if I was busy, and I'd say "Yeah," because I always was, and then he would say, "Let me see your hands." Then he would look at my hands and take them in his hands and see if there were calluses. Then he would just nod. He wouldn't say anything. . . . A very complicated guy. He was a very wonderful guy, and he stood for something we all remember very well.

Deetjen would not prove an easy man to work for, however, because the arduous standard he set for himself was difficult for most people to achieve, let alone sustain. He

LEFT: Deetjen's older sister Marie at a mountain cabin outside Bergen. Could it be the one Deetjen claimed he built, and for a time inhabited, as a boy of 12 or 13?
ABOVE, TOP: Letter from Norway, and Norwegian Stamp, year of Deetjen's birth.
ABOVE: Deetjen in front of a bronze Ibsen statue at the National Theater in Oslo, Norway, 1920.

Helen in the Deetjens' Castro Canyon campsite, with Helmuth's watercolors in the background.

had no patience with indolence. Some would say he had no patience at all. He felt that to live life in a meaningful way, one had to work—and work with passion. Deetjen, a trilingual intellectual who sought to learn from the masters, nevertheless maintained the playful wonder that Rilke says becomes part of the character of a person who learns a language later in life. His later language, English, was one he constantly played with. He balanced his gruff exterior with this compelling humor that few understood. The perfect enigmatic Norwegian troll for his chosen place in the woods!

There can be no doubt Deetjen's family worried about him when he left home. Even though he had traveled to Germany, France, and other countries, and had lived away from home for years, they must have sensed that the voyage to America had finality. In fact, though he wrote home, he never returned to Europe. However, Deetjen's two home languages, Norwegian and German, remained a refuge for him throughout life, a place he could retreat and few could follow. As a young man, he memorized German romantic poetry and, like most students of German, could recite Heine's "Die Lorelei" by heart, according to longtime friend and Inn guest Joe McLellan, who spoke German with Deetjen at dinner. In addition to Rilke and Heine, Deetjen also memorized short poems by Goethe, Schiller, and Nietzsche, and sang arias of many German operas—especially Mozart's *The Magic Flute*—in his unforgettable baritone fashion, smiling through every aria. He may have come to a new country but he didn't travel light. Europe never was more than a thought away, and he loved reminiscing about it with anyone who cared to join him.

HOME TURNS INN

When they completed the Inn just before World War II, the Deetjens decorated their new place with red fall foliage and invited the community to a housewarming. The bewildered

ABOVE: Poison oak in fall—the Deetjens unknowingly used it for decoration! LEFT: Ad for the opening of the Inn's restaurant, by Barbara Blake, placed June 1947 in Carmel's *Game and Gossip* magazine. Graphic of Big Sur Inn by Bruce Ariss. Courtesy of California Views, Pat Hathaway Collection.

Kent Seavey's *Big Sur Inn—A Brief History.* Courtesy Deetjen's, Inc. 1992.
Pen and Ink by Robin Coventry.

couple watched as their neighbors came but then left no sooner than they entered. The Deetjen walls were beautifully festooned—with poison oak! Clearly, they needed help with the décor. Some years later, they found just the answer. Enter: Barbara Blake.

Deetjen was not one to advertise. Far from it. He frequently discouraged people from coming to the Inn, as his friend Perry Newberry had done with the city of Carmel-by-the-Sea. When Newberry ran for mayor, it was on a no-growth, don't-vote-for-me-if you-want-sidewalks platform—similar to the way most Carmelites feel today. Deetjen left Carmel when the city began paving its streets, recalled Bob De Ford, but the pavement followed him to Big Sur, and with it, the traffic.

The Douglas iris in bloom in the canyon.

Once the Deetjen home became a haven for visitors, they leased part of their Inn to Barbara Blake. In the June 1947 issue of *Game and Gossip*, the Bruce Ariss publication, the Deetjens and Barbara Blake placed an announcement of the Opening, the Inn's first-known restaurant advertisement. Blake, then a recently widowed genteel Englishwoman, found her way to Big Sur just ten years after the opening of the Carmel–San Simeon Highway. She came at an opportune time, as highlighted in Kent Seavey's history booklet *Big Sur Inn—A Brief History*.

> She was taken by the natural beauty and spiritual quality of its setting. Mrs. Blake had experience in operating country inns and money to invest. . . . She leased the barn and expanded it with a shed-roofed wing to the south turning the place into a restaurant. Barbara Blake was responsible for the interior decoration of the Inn including purchase of the beautiful old bar, which came from the Smith family ranch at Westmere, and the English patternware table service so long in use at the Inn. Fortunately little has changed to alter the quiet ambience of the place. . . .

Who is Barbara Blake? For some reason, no one remembers. The photo tentatively identified as Blake, standing with Deetjen outside the restaurant, has had a question mark on it from its first day on display. Standing in front of the porch-turned-tearoom, with a teakettle above on a post, and looking better dressed than Big Sur folk, who else could she be? In any case, Blake appeared to make a lovely difference in a short period of time. The advertisement reads: "Barbara Blake (of the American Eagle Club, London). Opening June 8th, gives directions, then offers Breakfast, Lunch, Devonshire Tea, Dinner, Beer."

It was several years after Deetjen's death that Big Sur Inn acquired a beer-and-wine license, so it must be that no such requirement existed in 1947. Blake and the American Eagle Club, the organization the ad mentions, operated "The American Ambulance Great Britain." They used cars driven by Englishwomen, which in the postwar years formed the beginning of England's Red Cross. Through fundraising, the club was also

ABOVE: "One of the Largest Stein Collections in the West" boasts a 1950 ad—"In the Crook of the Road."
BELOW: Cornerstone tile, 1940, reminiscent of his voyage from Norway 15 years earlier.

loosely connected with AFS (American Field Service), the world's best known student-exchange program. Her role with the American Eagle Club never was defined but no doubt proved beneficial on many fronts during World War II. Likewise, Barbara Blake enhanced the operation and ambience of Big Sur Inn.

COMBINED TALENT—AND TORMENTS

At least as late as September 1950, the Deetjens, now without Blake, continued to advertise in *Game and Gossip*, but with an ad half the size.

The Deetjens' days appeared idyllic, and no doubt were for years, even with the difficulties typical of coastal mountain life. The hardest years for the couple came when the hardest work was done, when they had built, furnished, and decorated the Inn. Helen continued bargain hunting long after the Depression, but now she searched for antiques to sell in her antique shop. As Loet Vanderveen recalls, "She had a great eye for antiques." Deetjen also searched for materials, mainly wood and iron, with which to build. While she bought and sold antiques, he made furniture, wooden bowls, and other crafted goods to sell to travelers. He also fashioned decorative wrought-iron candleholders and other household items, many of which adorned the rustic rooms at the Inn and in the restaurant.

Throughout this period of productivity, the stress of living together in isolation hadn't time to surface. While driven by the same dream, they complemented one another, each having skills the other relied on. As with most couples, stress came on two fronts, internal and external. During the World War II years, Deetjen's native German garnered as much suspicion as one might expect in a small community. For all Big Sur's seemingly cosmopolitan aura, it retained a strong provincial aspect. The same small-town suspicions of newcomers applied, even in this scattered rural community. Then, too, the Deetjens had dogs in an area where cattle and sheep grazed. Neighbors could hardly approve of newcomers whose dogs at times chased the fat off their calves and lambs! Whatever exclusion the Deetjens may have felt, if in fact they had time to notice, could have contributed to the stress that began gnawing at their relationship.

Boasting "One of the West's Largest Stein Collections," and the beer to fill each, no doubt encouraged Deetjen to enjoy a bit more libation than he should. Similarly, Helen found her merrymaking in food, and as a diabetic, this would prove seriously detrimental to her health. In a period that should have been relatively stress-free came the greatest stress of all. By now the Deetjens were completely interdependent, but it was their other dependencies that might keep their relationship from reaching its full potential. The fabric of their common dream, once woven into reality, began to wear thin, to fray at the edges. This progression did not happen overnight but over decades; yet fulfilling moments certainly outweighed dysfunctional ones. Guests of the Inn would see only the extraordinarily beautiful home-like atmosphere, the inviting warmth, the charm, exactly what the Deetjens saw during their best hours. The welcoming atmosphere made the Inn a favorite breakfast and coffee stop that served a growing local community of artists, writers, and workers as it does today.

ABOVE: Deetjen with Big Sur Inn sign in 1945, the majority of his building completed.
BELOW: Deetjen's hands embraced and shaped every railing and post at the Inn, imparting his Scandinavian style on the otherwise ordinary cut of wood.

CREDO

My friend from Asia has powers and magic, he plucks a blue leaf from
   the young blue-gum
And gazing upon it, gathering and quieting
The God in his mind, creates an ocean more real than the ocean, the salt,
   the actual
Appalling presence, the power of the waters.
He believes that nothing is real except as we make it. I humbler have found
   in my blood
Bred west of Caucasus a harder mysticism.
Multitude stands in my mind but I think that the ocean in the bone vault is
   only
The bone vault's ocean: out there is the ocean's;
The water is the water, the cliff is the rock, come shocks and flashes of
   reality. The mind
Passes, the eye closes, the spirit is a passage;
The beauty of things was born before eyes and sufficient to itself; the
   heart-breaking beauty
Will remain when there is no heart to break for it.

Enchanted Room, Redwood Canopy. Photo by Noel Douglas Walling

Rocks at sunset—Pfeiffer Beach. Photo by Kodiak Greenwood.

three

AUTUMN EVENING

Though the little clouds ran southward still, the quiet autumnal
Cool of the late September evening
Seemed promising rain, rain, the change of the year, the angel
Of the sad forest. A heron flew over
With that remote ridiculous cry, "Quawk," the cry
That seems to make silence more silent. A dozen
Flops of the wing, a drooping glide, at the end of the glide
The cry, and a dozen flops of the wing.
I watched him pass on the autumn-colored sky; beyond him
Jupiter shone for evening star.
The sea's voice worked into my mood, I thought "No matter
What happens to men . . . the world's well made though."

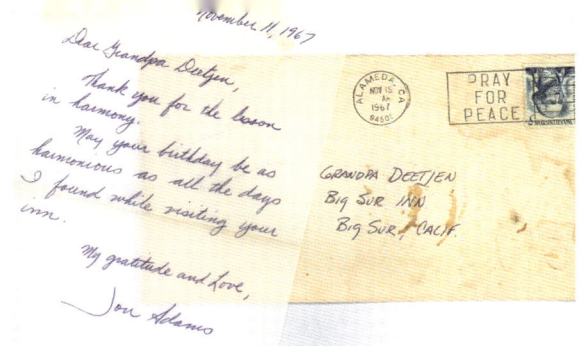

Not Breaking the Harmony

A WELL-MADE WORLD

Through his early Big Sur years, Deetjen's frequent walks to Carmel and Monterey put him in intimate contact with every aspect of coastal life. He learned his new land firsthand on these treks, seeing an abundance of sea life similar indeed to coastal Norway. He saw four-foot-tall herons on Lighthouse Flat, their six-foot wingspan wider than Deetjen's height. He observed these and other birds on both the Scandinavian and American west coasts—the egrets, Canada geese, golden eagles, and peregrine falcons. The west coasts of both California and Norway also share avocets, plovers, killdeer, stilts, sanderlings, sandpipers, phalaropes, willets, ruddy turnstones, pelicans, terns, and of course, the ever-present gulls. Deetjen missed his favorite game bird, now classified as threatened, the ptarmigan, a white grouse—and a Norwegian delicacy he recalled longingly throughout his life. Many varieties of birds in Castro Canyon, almost all of them non-game birds, were species that flourished around his Bergen home as well.

Abundant and familiar marine mammals also appeared on both shores. Seals, sea lions, dolphins, porpoises, and whales—some quite different, some the same—inhabited both the California and Norwegian coasts then as they do today. On these junkets in winter and spring, Deetjen noticed the migrating gray whales, and in summer, the blues and humpbacks. He said it was here that he saw his first sea otters, long hunted to near extinction but rediscovered in 1938. That same year, he and Helen married and began the ebb and flow of town trips necessary to build and later maintain the Inn. Helmuth left on foot two days ahead; Helen drove, with plans to bring home a host of antiques, first edition

FACING: Helen Deetjen's Antique Store fully functions in this early 1950s photo; in it, Deetjen smiles down on his eight cats (No mice here!). The sign reads, "Antiques OPEN, BOOKS—First Editions, ART, Paintings and Prints." The couple lived above in the room now called Top Antique. Courtesy of California Views, Pat Hathaway Collection.
ABOVE: A letter to Grandpa Deetjen, thanking him for "the lesson in harmony."

Interior of the Antique Shop, now called Grandpa's Room. Courtesy of California Views, Pat Hathaway Collection.

books, and other collectibles. The Deetjen Antique Shop also sold paintings and prints.

Don McQueen, board member for the nonprofit Deetjen's Incorporated, moved to Big Sur in 1939 at age 11, and remembers working on areas of the Inn almost from its inception. He recalled a typical Deetjen town trip: "He would take off two days ahead of time and walk into town. They had a green Dodge pick-up truck, and Helen would drive to town. They would buy stuff and load it, used stuff from Goodwill. She'd drive, and he'd come walking back in a day or so."

PREPARING TO BUILD: "I DON'T BREAK THE HARMONY. . ."

While he built, Deetjen observed a timeless rhythm that contributed to the Inn's feeling of integrity and to the unusual blending of nature with man-made materials. What he saw and heard continually was nature's industry: the migrations, the nurturing of young, the preparing for winter. His hammer tapped with the enterprising woodpeckers, flickers, and sapsuckers. His saw kept to the rhythm of rapid breathing. Each hand tool echoed and faded in the canyon with nature's own eternal sounds. The main power used in building the Inn was manpower, nearly all of it supplied by Deetjen himself.

"I don't break the harmony of all delicate things," Deetjen said of the Inn one evening at dinner. Though his Bergen home was palatial by comparison, the Inn Deetjen built came to be his castle—and more. It became, and remains, a spiritual haven, a sanctuary for thousands, and an odd parallel to his father's far more ornate, self-built home-turned-dormitory. Helmuth had seen his elaborate family home built from scratch as a youth and knew from the beginning how he would proceed with his own home. His skill as a civil engineer and enterprising surveyor, coupled with the work he had done alongside his father and on buildings in Europe and the United States, served him well when he encountered problems. When Deetjen was still in his twenties, 1920 Norwegian Nobel Laureate Knut Hamsun hired him as a surveyor. Though Henry Miller emulated his writing and Thomas Mann, among numerous others, admired his work, Hamsun's support of Germany cost him his reputation and property. Hamsun hired Deetjen during the height of his literary career, twenty years before his fall from favor in Europe.

Though no documentation confirms it, Deetjen reportedly worked on a port facility on the Gold Coast of Africa before coming back to Norway and immigrating to the United States. In any case, his background more than prepared him for the tasks ahead. Still, filling and stabilizing the land was not a task for the faint of heart.

Deetjen's early interest and training in art helped him visualize and plan the distinctive series of rustic dwellings and shops reminiscent of his Bergen heritage. Neither his sketches nor watercolors remain, but they served their purpose. In time, those miniatures would take on the look of a small Norwegian village; but the challenges then, as now, of building in Big Sur were considerable. The Castro Canyon acreage came with powerful advantages and disadvantages. On the positive side, Deetjen had nature's own construction materials, water to mix cement, and lumber from downed trees. Both these essentials lay in close proximity to the building site. However, Big Sur's topographic vagaries and its often severe weather offset those advantages. The key to completing the Inn lay in his knowledge, dedication, determination, and resourcefulness.

THE DEETJEN VERNACULAR ARCHITECTURE

"It was a 45-foot-deep hole," Deetjen said in his baritone voice and heavy Norwegian accent, referring to the part of Castro Canyon he chose for his workshop and first home. "It had to be filled by hand." He gave that mischievous smile and added, "It was a dimple in the planet." Deetjen would need to overcome some serious engineering problems before he could frame the Barn, as he aptly called the first of their many board-and-batten buildings. Filling and stabilizing the mobile Big Sur ground provided just one of many challenges he would need to conquer before constructing his workshop, the building

ABOVE: Grandpa Deetjen's bells hang in numerous places around the Inn. These top the gate at the entrance to Castro Canyon.
BELOW: X-panel doors open into the Champagne Room.

that would in time house the restaurant, office, and attic, where some of the help later slept bunkhouse style. Initially, the Deetjens kept milk goats in the north end of the Barn on the porch area adjacent to the workshop. He built with versatility in mind, not knowing how their needs would change.

When the camping phase of construction came to a close and the time came to locate building materials, Deetjen's resourcefulness compensated for the disadvantages most builders encountered during the Great Depression. Not only did he have a canyon of downed and partly harvested redwood trees for building, but also his trips to town netted doors, doorknobs, hinges, handles, and galvanized pipes. Fellow Norwegian Knut Hovden, builder of Hovden Cannery (now the site of the Monterey Bay Aquarium), may have provided Deetjen with contacts for supplies. He likely salvaged from abandoned buildings around Cannery Row, made famous by John Steinbeck and Ed Ricketts, when "Doc" and Steinbeck's real characters, ultimately fictionalized, still lived there.

And nails! If you could find nails during the Depression, they cost more than most

The restaurant, looking rather more like a wild west facade, housed Helen's original Antique Shop, Helmuth's workshop, and their upstairs home. Two of their faithful dogs lounge in the sun. Customers entered through a small mudroom, now the restaurant's Porch. Courtesy of Deetjen's Inc.

owner-builders could afford, and a short time later World War II would place most metals at a premium. For a time, even pennies were made of aluminum to conserve copper for the war effort. "I had to straighten every nail," Deetjen recalled, shaking his hand as if remembering a hammered finger. Helmuth was as proficient at arranging deals and scavenging otherwise useless items as Helen was at bargaining for antiques. They transported most of their bargains over newly opened Highway One. Not so with the windows. These reclaimed items Deetjen had packed over the Santa Lucia Mountains by mule. He was particularly proud of that find: "I bought every window in the place for five dollars," he boasted. The windows wound through the mountains from King City, miraculously arriving intact. Few of the panes have ever needed replacing, and their wavy, antique appearance still mesmerizes visitors more than sixty-five years later. Guests gazing through them never imagine the energy, luck, and determination required in bringing the panels over the twisting, steep trail from Salinas Valley to the Big Sur Coast. Deetjen almost made it sound as though finding a place to put each windfall window became part of his building plan. Indeed, every room has more than sufficient available light when power outages occur, which can be often and lengthy during Big Sur winters.

With their need to accommodate the increasing number of visitors, Deetjen would just complete work on one project when another surfaced. The Hay Loft, the building adjacent to their first home, came next. In a short time, that building shifted from an agrarian function to serving visitors. To avoid confusion here, the Inn has two "Fireplace Rooms," the first in the Restaurant and the other in a guest room in the Hay Loft. In addition to that Fireplace Room, the Hay Loft houses Little Room, Petite Cuisine,

ABOVE: The wavy antique glass windows Deetjen bought in the Depression era remain part of the Inn's mesmerizing charm.

BELOW: Deetjen family crest, carved by his Norwegian friend Mike Anderson, whose work appears at the Inn and at Stanton Center Maritime Museum in Monterey, California.

BELOW: Deetjen carefully constructed The Gallo Wall, shown behind Chateau Fiasco, to function as a retaining wall. Without his direction, the help left the top of the wall a jumble of jugs.
RIGHT: Part of the Hayloft building, a corner of the Honeymoon Room.
FACING: Chateau Fiasco, built during the Bay of Pigs debacle, has two explanations for its odd name. Perhaps both apply. Beneath Chateau Fiasco is Edy's Room, named for Edith O'Ryan, the Deetjen's accountant of many years.

Honeymoon Room, and the Van Gogh Room, reputed to have once displayed a Van Gogh original. The Inn would have been a safer place for original artwork than most of Europe during the war, and Deetjen did enjoy close ties to Europe's bohemian art world for many years. No one can confirm a temporary Vincent placement, but the room does house Van Gogh prints.

Each of the five rooms in the Hay Loft has its own intrinsic quality, all sharing two airy bathrooms. The memorabilia, photographs, and artwork that adorn the hall and rooms give each one a comfortable, secure, home-like feeling. Likewise, Deetjen's distinctive built-in bookcases, shelves, and mantelpieces invite the placement of personal keepsakes, some of these left by Inn guests but most left from the days of Mrs. Deetjen's Antique Store.

Near the Hay Loft are three rooms just behind the current Restaurant, the upper floor built toward the end of Deetjen's construction period. Here, against the hill, he constructed the Franklin Room, so named for its cozy Franklin stove; Edy's Room, named for Edith O'Ryan, Helen and Helmuth's longtime accountant and friend who had for years called the room home; and the Chateau Fiasco, the playful name given to the upstairs room that had a chandelier made of Chianti wine bottles. Venetian glassblowers turned bottles with even a slight flaw into a common flask or fiasco. One vintner wrapped these bottles with straw to cover the inferior glass product and the Chianti inside became wildly popular—and here, at least, made an uncommon chandelier. However, to challenge the tale's veracity, a second version of this Castro Canyon allegory leads straight to another Castro—Fidel! Deetjen named the upstairs expansion of the Franklin Room and Edy's Room, completed in 1961, to commemorate the Bay of Pigs invasion! Whether politically

or physically inspired (or both), Chateau Fiasco remains a favorite with guests, a tree-shrouded, second-story room with a lovely deck overlooking the activities of the restaurant and the main part of the Inn, as does the deck of the nearby Fireplace Room.

Behind Chateau Fiasco lay another fiasco of sorts. Deetjen let nothing go to waste. He once pointed to the three-foot retaining wall built of empty gallons of Gallo wine, each neatly stacked and keeping winter rains running into the bottles instead of into the rooms. Seemed to work. Mud was used as mortar between the bottles as well as filling them; but atop Deetjen's orderly wall lay jade-colored jugs, not broken but strewn randomly and without purpose. The construction of the wall ceased for no apparent reason. Asked what happened, Deetjen made a sweeping gesture and replied, "This is where the help took over."

FINISHING AND FURNISHING THE INN

Throughout the time Deetjen built the Inn, he built tables, chairs, beds, benches, dressers, and other artistically rendered furniture reminiscent of his native Norway. From redwood burl, he formed bowls and other items to sell, finding the canyon redwood an easy wood to carve. On days when weather prevented him from working outside, he worked on furniture for the rooms, much of it functional built-in cabinets, shelving, bed frames, and drawers, as had been his style when he built in Carmel before coming to Big Sur.

When materials were available, he forged wrought-iron candelabras and other small items to sell. Most of his work he sold or bartered, but some remains at the Inn. A furniture buyer could easily transport Deetjen's benches, chairs, and most of his tables in a car or pick-up truck because each creation came apart, and the buyer could reassemble them easily. The family table and benches, Deetjen's most notable pieces, still grace the Restaurant's Family Room where Deetjen dined each evening. These he made without nails or screws. Instead, smooth solid pegs have held the benches and table together since 1939.

He used a natural oil finish, a formula unfortunately not put in writing. Two of the three ingredients were lemon oil and pure tung oil. He also rubbed these into his hand-carved fruit and salad bowls and, later on, chopping blocks in the kitchen. He never used varnish or lacquer on the surface of anything he made and scoffed at the idea, saying that if you finished it right, you wouldn't have to do it over and the luster would last for ten years. Varathane formulas had yet to be invented when Deetjen did his woodworking, but it's likely he would have rejected those or any of the polymers that have come along since. He preferred natural products.

All the time Helmuth built shelves and nooks, Helen brought home antiques and

ABOVE: Downstairs from Chateau Fiasco, the Franklin Room and Edy's Room make up the rest of that complex.
BELOW: The redwood mortise and tenon benches Deetjen built employed no nails or screws, but were joined together solely with pegs, making it easy for the traveler to pack the pieces in the car and to reassemble them at home. Deetjen made the Family Table and its matching benches in this manner.

48 BIG SUR INN: THE DEETJEN LEGACY

LEFT: Deetjen fashioned many redwood burl bowls for the seasonal tourist trade. The concave burl shape lent itself to that purpose, and was an especially strong and pleasingly decorative part of the tree. Courtesy of Bob DeFord.
BELOW: Candleholders like this one attest to Deetjen's skill as a blacksmith. He made many items of metal, but preferred woodworking.

astutely chosen bargains with which to populate the shelf space, alongside Helmuth's handmade bowls and candleholders.

Deetjen went on to build what he called The Castle, the complex that was in fact his castle until he died. The space currently available as Grandpa's Room was first the site of Mrs. Deetjen's Antique Store, which needed more storage space because of the seasonal nature of Big Sur businesses and Helen's tendency to hoard. Helmuth continued adding rooms to the store and adjacent storage rooms, forming what are now Grandpa's Room, and the Antique Apartment. Those downstairs rooms remained un-rented and were packed with artifacts as long as Deetjen was alive, though four years after Helen's death, he did have a friend, Eduardo Tirella, begin organizing the room that had remained empty since Mrs. Deetjen stopped selling antiques in about 1960. During this renovation, Tirella was tragically killed in an auto accident, run over by heiress Doris Duke in 1966, leading to a much-publicized civil trial; Tirella had been Duke's interior designer in New

Not Breaking the Harmony 49

Once the Deetjen's Antique Shop and upstairs home, this quaint area now houses The 13th Room, Top Antique, and Grandpa's Room.

Jersey. Deetjen locked the rooms after that, seldom allowing anyone inside.

The Deetjens called the Top Antique home (or Castle) for many years. From that location, they could survey the entire Inn, but best of all they still enjoyed the ocean view they had above the workshop. They remained there until Mrs. Deetjen's illness caused them to move downstairs and distribute the Antique Store artifacts between the storage rooms, the Restaurant, and what is now the Reading Room, a common space for guests to relax. The Deetjens' upstairs room, the Top Antique, became a rental.

Deetjen placed bunk beds in the complex that adjoins the Antique area and called it the Hostelry. The ladder to the top bunk, now beautifully refinished and mounted with care on the wall, has the look of useful art. Originally, he intended the room for friends and stranded (or broke) guests. Now a part of the Antique Apartment, the Hostelry rented separately for many years. In the 60s, when the Hostelry bunks rented for $2 a night, vines grew through the bathroom window, and to flush the toilet, a sign instructed the guest to fill the bucket in the shower and pour it into the tank. Seasoned occupants of that room learned the basics of plumbing. They also learned to plan ahead!

Next to the Hostelry was the comparatively elegant New Room. All the rooms in that complex overlook the canyon, as does the next building, a two-story that houses the Chalet upstairs and the Champagne Room below. The most distant part of the Inn, as Deetjen himself built it, is known as the Creek House, a two-story dwelling with views of Castro Creek. Families often rent Upper Creek and Lower Creek together.

Later additions, those following Deetjen's death, are adjacent to Castro Creek and, for the most part, have become rentals expanded from utility or staff rooms such as Castro Canyon, Stokes Cabin, and Faraway, all built in Deetjen's rustic style.

The tireless Deetjen built another two houses on top of the grassy upper reaches of their land—the Top House, and the Goat House. Don and Glenn McQueen laid the pipeline to each house. Both these buildings needed a different treatment in order to resist the driving rains that can force their way through walls and under eaves. Deetjen built them with timbers strong enough to withstand the south winds that propel winter storms hard against the land. He took advantage of the sun's warmth but whitewashed the buildings to reflect the intense sun of the summer's heat. For a time, Deetjen tried living at the Top House, but he found that he was unable to keep an eye on the workers and soon moved back to the Inn.

ABOVE: A fleeting glance inside the Z-paneled Dutch doors reveals the Antique Apartment, with its cozy wood stove. Located next to The 13th Room, the Antique Apartment now incorporates what once was The Hostelry, making it a small rustic suite.

LEFT: This bird's eye view map shows the Inn as Deetjen envisioned it when he stood on a trail overlooking the tiny relocated Norwegian village. Artwork by Jane Chanteau. Courtesy of the Big Sur Inn Preservation Foundation.

The Deetjens rented the upland buildings to various artists and workers over the years. Both the Top House and the Goat House became and now remain staff housing.

Because the Deetjens had camped on-site, they knew the sun angles and how to build for passive solar warmth. The all-important placement of windows can cut down on the need for firewood. As winter's sun angle dipped, long warm rays reached across his workshop and later the restaurant. Over time, lovely foliage has blocked some of Deetjen's solar strategy. Years later the Inn, under Ed Gardien's management, installed rustic Jotul Norwegian wood-burning stoves. Deetjen built the ceiling beams of the workshop low in order to take advantage of the heat from the only fireplace they had; warmth from the fireplace would rise to aid the passive solar in their upstairs quarters.

The restaurant fireplace had its own bit of serendipity. The simple design of the bricks against the rich redwood gives a sense of peacefulness to all those who enter the room. The Inn without it seems unimaginable, but Deetjen teased, "Our fireplace was on the floor." He went on to say that the current floor of the restaurant Fireplace Room and Family Room started as brick. Before he could get the mortar mixed and poured, a cold snap changed his plans. Don McQueen said that as a youngster, he helped frame and

build the Fireplace Room, and that he could point out mistakes he made in the process. After several chilly days, while Don did woodworking, Deetjen rearranged the bricks, fashioning them into the brick hearth and mantel that has warmed family, friends, and strangers for more than sixty-five years.

A TOWN TRIP

The Inn might have had quite a different appearance had Deetjen used more power and less hand tools. Once power did come, Don McQueen installed all of the original wiring at the Inn. McQueen also felt that the introduction of electricity ruined Big Sur in many ways, disrupting the silence. The first electric power came down the coast in 1949, the same year it came to Carmel Point; however, in Big Sur it only served the coast to Point Sur Light Station, which had been oil-powered since its opening in 1889. The power to serve the majority of Big Sur came in 1953, according to Deetjen's neighbor Bill Post, whose ranch has since become the world-renowned Post Ranch Inn. Post recalled that residential telephone service came the same year. Today, some parts of the coast still use solar or generator power or a combination. Power became a necessity when the U.S. Navy leased land from El Sur Ranch and built Point Sur Oceanographic Research Station. Established in 1957 as a top secret Cold War facility, the Navy designed the base as a listening station to detect Soviet nuclear submarines. Proximity of the base to the U.S. Coast Guard's Point Sur Light Station meant information could be shared in an emergency, but

FACING TOP: Top House interior, c. 1944.
FACING BELOW: A rare old color slide shows the Inn, Antique Shop, and home of the indefatigable Deetjens, the Bells of Bergen on the gate still shining, the redwood still relatively new, and a properly set sundial in place. The old buckboard wagonseat, shown here, still sat outside Grandpa's Room for at least another 40 years. In addition to Antiques, the sign reads Weaving (Helen's) and Woodcraft (Helmuth's). In the background, the Deetjens' truck awaits its driver.
ABOVE: Deetjen pauses from work on the Top House and Goat House, with a view of the Santa Lucia Mountains, headlands, and ocean. Courtesy of California Views, Pat Hathaway Collection.
LEFT: View of the Restaurant from Mrs. Deetjen's favorite window, in what is now Top Antique, 1950.

Though known for trail building, Deetjen also planted trees. Stretching south of Point Sur Light Station is the forest of Monterey Cypress that he, with Walt, and Frank Trotter and "Pop" Crawford, planted at the request of the El Sur Ranch owner. Recalling the size of the newly planted "forest," Grandpa said, "It looked like the world's largest carrot patch." He watched their growth through the years as he walked to town. Photo courtesy of David Spence and the Beachcomber Inn, Pacific Grove, California.

the two facilities remained autonomous and basically unrelated. The purpose of the lighthouse, then and now, was as an aid to navigation. The Navy decommissioned its base in 1984 and the state now uses a portion for housing. The state of California and volunteers from Central Coast Lighthouse Keepers currently operate the lighthouse as Point Sur State Historic Park.

Around 1939, the owner of the ranchland that borders the Point Sur Light Station hired Deetjen, along with "the Trotter boys," as he called them (Walt and Frank Trotter) and Pop Crawford, to plant Monterey cypress trees above the beach south of Point Sur. The planting took about a week. The rancher needed to establish a windbreak to help keep the sand out of his milk buckets and other dairy products. The northernmost part of that expansive alluvial flat, now part of Andrew Molera State Park, for many years had commercially produced large quantities of Monterey Jack cheese. Wind not only whipped across the sand and into milk buckets, but it sent a yellow haze into the sky for miles down the coast. The cypress trees helped, but grass and brush seeds scattered by birds, wild animals, cattle, and wind may have done even more to hold down the airborne sand. Before the grasses and other vegetation grew along the flat, the stretch of land from Highway One to the base of the lighthouse rock was a broad sand-swept tombolo that in the recent past would render "The Rock" an island.

The Monterey cypress forest Deetjen, Crawford and the Trotters planted still skirts the coast and stands between 50 and 75 feet tall, but when newly planted, the thick blanket of baby cypress trees first stood only 8 to 10 inches high. Deetjen said, "It looked like the world's largest carrot patch." The healthy forest seen in the aerial photo continually reseeds itself, as other coastal cypress plantings do, marking former and current homesteads along the coast. Deetjen knew the speed with which these trees grew because the street in Carmel where he built one home on San Antonio Avenue had a tall canopy of cypresses, most of which he also planted.

CARMEL AND CARMEL POINT

The Deetjen-built Carmel home between 10th and 11th on San Antonio Avenue, though more polished than the Inn, still maintained Helmuth's Norwegian architectural style. Its cozy personal spaces provided many locations for its occupants to place photos and mementos. From the built-in bookshelves and cabinetry to corner nooks and deep-set shelves, Deetjen's characteristic home design welcomed everyone who entered. The San Antonio dwelling had first been a caretaker's cottage. Its wide French doors opened onto a deck over the garage, causing Deetjen to dub it The Hangover House.

Exacting, alluring workmanship is uncommon in large homes, but is rare indeed in a tiny, warm one-bedroom cottage—the roof joists, beams with diamond patterns, notches and angled edges all speak of meticulous attention to detail. The long driveway, lined with rock Deetjen brought from a local quarry, led to the intimate dwelling, one that even entering day after day held an element of surprise and delight. It's the sort of contemplative place that people long to find. Asked about the time he took to carve the details into each beam, railing, and post, Deetjen shrugged as though the time meant nothing, and design everything.

Deetjen's skilled hands graced a second Carmel dwelling, the Bay View Avenue house on Carmel Point that he and Helen called home before moving to Big Sur. Inside and out, you could recognize the smooth, carefully carved railings similar to the posts and railings at the Inn. The rambling two-story home with a basement has the unmistakable look of Deetjen's craftsmanship throughout. His built-in storage, beds, drawers, shelves, corner nooks, arched cabinets, and sculpted rails demonstrated Deetjen's design and fine woodworking capability. The upstairs rooms had a cypress-framed ocean view, one similar to the second-story living quarters they planned and later occupied in Big Sur.

His secure, massive wrought-iron hinges, locks, and other hardware at the Bay View house attested to his skill as a blacksmith. The one-of-a-kind hardware gave their home a warm Old World appearance throughout, with uniquely hand-forged fixtures in the kitchen as well.

Colin E. Kuster, son of Theodore Kuster (the first husband of Una Jeffers), lived a short distance from Helen and Helmuth on Carmel Point, and described the house and the couple in amazing detail. He said all the Carmel Point neighbors knew each other.

ABOVE, TOP: In Carmel, on San Antonio Avenue, between 10th and 11th, beneath a canopy of cypresses he also planted, Deetjen built a cozy one bedroom cottage, with appealing details. ABOVE: Deetjen packed the small cottage with unique, functional storage spaces such as the ones shown here in the dining area. Courtesy of California Views, Pat Hathaway Collection.

They were known as "Deetjen and Miss Haight" he related in a letter to the Inn. His recollection of Eight Bells, from the lot location to the house description, is blue-print crisp.

The Bay View house had in it the beginnings of some humor later found in a storage room at Big Sur Inn. On a floor beam above the low steps heading to the basement, Deetjen stenciled the letters: "DUCK." Several steps later, another low spot, and more stenciled letters: "DUCK, AGAIN!" Back at the Inn, Deetjen painted "DUCK" above the low storage-room entrance of the Duck House (under the Hay Loft). Inside, on a beam (never where guests might peer) the next sign read, "DUCK, YOU!"

DOWN THE COAST

Had Deetjen stayed in Carmel, it's easy to imagine his skill rivaling the best builders on the Monterey Peninsula. He had the talent, technique, and creativity to build whatever he chose. Deetjen had the spirit of a poet; his enigmatic phrases, the parables he used, and that same ability to play with language was also apparent when he built. He was a poet with wood, finding hidden surprises and layered meanings in it beneath the surface. Likewise with hammer, anvil, and iron, he heated, bent, and shaped objects as a wordsmith kindles emotion.

If what he built seems unassuming, it is always that way when work comes direct from the heart. He used all he had, putting his love into the Inn with the pounding of every nail. What we see and feel in this place, the raw constructive instinct of humanity, is all that's worth striving for: doing our best with what we've been given.

The Big Sur Coast is a harsh and powerful place. Deetjen gave it warmth. In our current unsustainable city lifestyle, it's important to look at the peacefulness the Deetjens

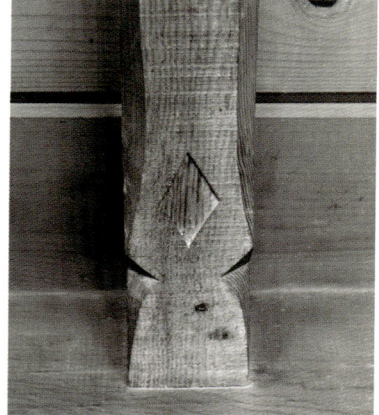

ABOVE, RIGHT: Beam details exhibit the careful craftsmanship of some of Deetjen's most distinctive work.
ABOVE: In what he called The Hangover House, Deetjen carved each beam with a diamond pattern, saying, "It takes away the mechanical look." Deetjen always preferred hand-carved timbers to machine-milled, which is what gives the Inn its hand-made warmth. Courtesy of California Views, Pat Hathaway Collection.

created and try to regain the sanity people feel when they come here. With simple natural materials, the Inn displays "intentional rusticity," as publisher Gibbs Smith called the weathered retreat that is Big Sur Inn. In a world that seems to be asking us to understand our surroundings, this is not a road map to ignore. Deetjen's teaches how to transform the uninhabitable into someplace safe and cozy. The Inn gives the traveling urban public the taste of a Big Sur home—because initially, it was one.

Big Sur artist and publisher Reed Cripe says that Deetjen's gave him the inspiration to build his board-and-batten home in Big Sur. Cripe was struck by the integrity and warmth the Inn offered, "the organic way it grew." Deetjen "grew the Inn out of the canyon. It grew from what was needed, not planned," he observed. Taking his cue from Deetjen, Cripe was able to find used materials to incorporate in his own home. His doors came from the Last Chance Mercantile, a store at the Marina landfill where trash and treasure blend. "We have a 1920 cook stove and use it for every meal. We're off the grid."

Internationally known architect Mickey Muennig, designer of the award-winning Post Ranch Inn in Big Sur, is among breakfast regulars at Deetjen's, and has stayed in the Little Room, Grandpa's Room, and Chateau Fiasco. Muennig's imaginative luxury rooms bear little resemblance to the simplicity of the Inn, yet he says of Deetjen's: "It had quite a big influence on my character, and the way I live." Muennig had already established a reputation as an avant-garde architect before moving to Big Sur in 1971. He met Grandpa Deetjen, and for Muennig, being at the Inn was more of a personal connection than anything else. "Just from his actions and the way he lived and all . . . I came out here because I liked the lifestyle of the people, the way they lived." Grandpa exemplified that for him, and though there was little Muennig could learn about architecture from Deetjen, they do share in common the ability to build without "breaking the harmony" of the land, to blend gently with nature, and to build in entirely different ways—only what honors this magnificent coast.

Hampton Fancher, actor, screenwriter, and director, wrote a 1957 impression of the Inn, recalling when he stopped for directions to Henry Miller's Partington Ridge home, not realizing that Deetjen had built it.

> Deetjen will never let me forget him, not so much because of anything he actually did or said, but maybe because of his simple native presence. I was 18 and all of him and where he was, was so absolute and new. First time maybe I thought I'd met a man who was comfortable and sure in living outside the world where others had no choice but to live. . . . I fancy now that he was a Robinson Crusoe who knew well how to put found objects to use. . . . Most of all, I think he loved those who loved most authentically the place he'd made. There is maybe where the center of his love exhausted and revived itself.

ABOVE, TOP: Inside the Bay View house, Deetjen's ample storage and distinctive hand-shaped posts and railing, make the house both attractive and practical. ABOVE: Deetjen's handyman Stokes Evans views the back entrance of the rambling Bay View House. Courtesy of Deetjen's, Inc.

ON THE CLIFF

Do you remember, dear, that little house
Built hard against the high cliff's ragged brows
Over the emerald ocean's level floor
Where we were sitting, while the quick day wore
To sunset? Ah, how swiftly the day passed,
Our day, our one sweet day that would not last,
Altho' we did not see the sun go down,
Nor knew till darkness that the sun was gone,
Because our eyes were blind, while my lips drank
Oblivious love at yours.

                              But the sun sank;
Nor all our urgent wishing had the power
To lengthen out our day by one poor hour.

Soberanes at Sunset. Photo by Kodiak Greenwood.

four

THE HOUSE-DOG'S GRAVE

(Haig, an English Bulldog)

I've changed my ways a little: I cannot now
Run with you in the evenings along the shore,
Except in a kind of dream: and you, if you dream a moment,
You see me there.

So leave awhile the paw-marks on the front door
Where I used to scratch to go out or in,
And you'd soon open; leave on the kitchen floor
The marks of my drinking-pan.

I cannot lie by your fire as I used to do
On the warm stone,
Nor at the foot of your bed: no, all the nights through
I lie alone.

But your kind thought has laid me less than six feet
Outside your window where firelight so often plays,
And where you sit to read—and I fear often grieving for me—
Every night your lamplight lies on my place.

You, man and woman, live so long it is hard
To think of you ever dying.
A little dog would get tired living so long.
I hope that when you are lying

Under the ground like me your lives will appear
As good and joyful as mine.
No, dears, that's too much hope: you are not so well cared for
As I have been,

And never have known the passionate undivided
Fidelities that I knew.
Your minds are perhaps too active, too many-sided. . . .
But to me you were true.

You were never masters, but friends. I was your friend.
I loved you well, and was loved. Deep love endures
To the end and far past the end. If this is my end,
I am not lonely. I am not afraid. I am still yours.

Room for Inspiration

The creation of the Inn came from Whitman's poem "Song of the Redwood-Tree." Perhaps because poetry inspired Deetjen, the Inn he built inspires nearly all who enter it. Deetjen built a place for the spirit to rest, not just the body. If it feels like an artist's colony, it is because from the beginning, the Deetjens welcomed working artists and their pets. They created what hardly fits the definition of a hotel or motel. Every corner of the Inn welcomes guests—regulars and newcomers alike.

So it follows that guests who enter these rooms find their own inspiration in this security, and whether for a few lines or page after page, they spill their thoughts into the journals inside each room, journals that stay in place year after year. In the '50s, perhaps earlier, the Deetjens kept a journal of sorts, a bound unlined volume on the coffee bar in the reception area. Visitors and locals alike placed thoughts and thank you notes, sketches, quotes, and flashes of inspiration in this one large guestbook.

The built-in love and warmth of the Inn inspires reverence and trust, as did all the animals that inhabited the Inn when the Deetjens were alive. What could make you feel more at home than a pet? Even a borrowed one! In the Deetjen days, if you did not bring a dog or cat with you, it was easy to find a surrogate. In fact, it was hard not to find a cat. An open window was an open invitation. Nearly all the Deetjen dogs could be trusted. Nearly. Errant pooches, whether the Inn's or a guest's, spent moments incarcerated across from Deetjen's room, well cared for. The rental of the Jai Ram Jail suite of pooch rooms: $1.00 per day. The Deetjens treated their pets with the affection they would children. As though trying to write in journals of their own, the dogs' pawed messages, gouged in the doors, show that

FACING: Red Berries and Top Antique.
ABOVE, TOP: Guest book—1956.
ABOVE: The Jai Ram Jail for wayward dogs, across from Grandpa's Room, rented for one dollar per day. Courtesy of Big Sur Inn Preservation Foundation.

Antique Apartment interior.

reverence and trust remain.

In the '60s and '70s, Inn guests frequently left a favorite book, one they might well find in the same place years later or in a different room, often read and lovingly cared for. People inscribed many of the books they left. The Inn now keeps published books in a separate reading room for all to enjoy. Before the advent of in-room journals, guests left messages on the backs of framed pictures if they had nowhere else to write. Once journals evolved and found their way into each room, guests no longer resorted to such eccentric measures. If one is here, it's easy to write, to feel part of something grander, to connect. Guests often felt the need to leave other small treasures or to send them. One journal entry mentions a guest sending a fresh rose wreath to the Inn. The journal writer reveals that she found it years later, now as a dried arrangement.

In countless journals of many sizes, mostly bought by guests and left on tables or bookshelves in each room, travelers leave solved and unsolved dilemmas, partial and complete poems, quoted prose, scriptures and sketches. It would be impossible, if not an intrusion, to reproduce all the pages, but they remain there for the reading, glimpses into traveling souls, generous shared delights, invitations. What a rare find, these private musings, signed and unsigned, placed on public display. Seldom does a guest miss the chance to peer into each volume and add at least a thought to the collection. The journals range from guileless observations to sophisticated references, with grammatical conventions from precise to e-mail style. As in Shakespearean times, the scribes at Deetjen's are unencumbered by dictionaries and spelling rules. Varied penmanship keeps one's eyes adjusting, entry by entry. Script runs the gamut from perfect blueprint style to near graffiti. The variety of ink colors, sketches, and foreign languages further enhance the texture of each book.

The tone of the journals differs from room to room. Reflections left in the Creek House, some distance from the main part of the Inn itself, differ from those closer to the Inn's center. The interactive musings written in the Honeymoon Room or The Fireplace Room, graphic in some cases, often share intimate feelings between couples or insightful family relationships. Conversely, the Petite Cuisine, a cozy monastic room with a single bed, inspires more careful introspection—and at times personal revelation.

"I drive again past The Big Sur Inn where just a few nights ago I surrendered to its beauty," writes poet Stephen John Kalinich. He recalled moments of his stay in these lines:

From the Big Sur Inn
by Stephen John Kalinich

You must find it again
in your own authenticity.
There is a stripping down
of ones being
reduced to a solitary soul
walking alone
gliding and floating
through the images
of light shimmering
upon the Ocean—
Around every corner
is a memory
Vitality longs
for re-Emergence
Longs to fill the empty vessels—
of the inhabitants
of the native mystery.
The enigma of a place
Old buildings

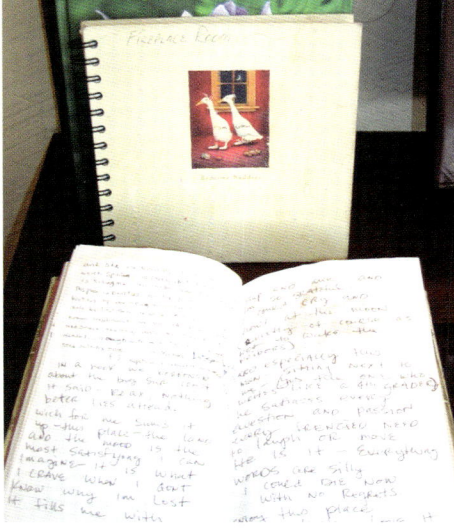

The Fireplace Room Journals.

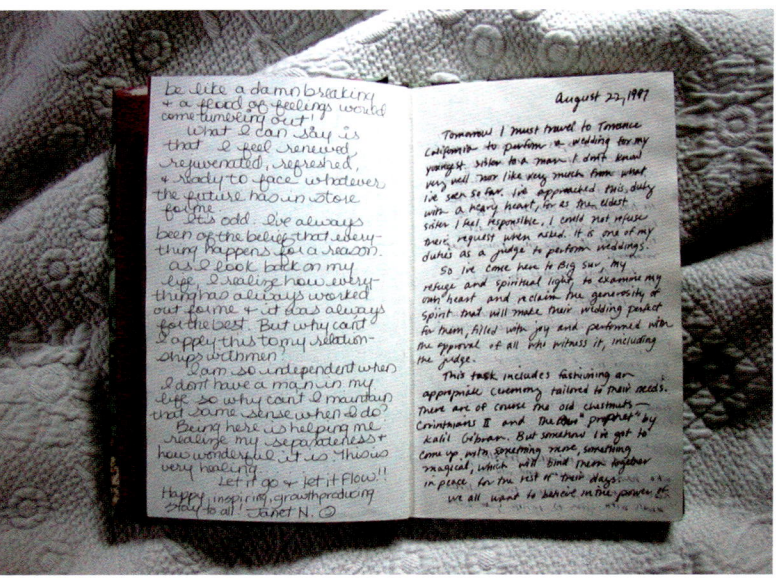

FOUND POEMS

The journal samplings that follow come from Petite Cuisine, Little Room, Honeymoon Room, Fireplace Room, Van Gogh, Chateau Fiasco, Creek House, Antique Apartment, and the Top House, but most of all, they come from the heart. They fall in no particular order, single lines for the most part, pulled from sincere, sometimes lengthy, realizations. With enough time, one could categorize them into themes, perhaps seeing distinct differences from room to room, season to season. One can look at this collection from many perspectives.

As editor, I found no temptation to add to what the writers here share. The words fall as they do. If words are missing, the standard ellipses replace them. Most of the titles come from part of a journal entry.

Poet Patrice Vecchione gives the following definition of a found poem: You find the words from somewhere outside yourself—dinner menu, road sign, essay, story, poem—connect them to other found words, phrases, and sentences. Add some of your own, and voila, a poem.

What follows here says more about the Inn than any one writer alone could impart. These aggregates of small gems, selected from scores of pages in more than thirty journals, encourage each guest to continue the Inn's tradition of sharing life's poignant and joyous sensations, hopes, knowledge, and observations. In the following found poems, each solitary writer becomes a mystery that solves itself when one recognizes these words as the collective human spirit.

ABOVE, RIGHT: Petite Cuisine Journal.
ABOVE: A converted gas lamp has been lighting the way to the Hayloft building for over 50 years.

Speaking from the Heart of the Rooms

Deetjen's is the childhood we have never had, but remember.
It is when I open my arms that I am safest, enveloped in your love,
flowing into the stony ribs of the coast.
Returning to Papa Deetjen's is like coming home . . .
The deep quietness opens our minds.
The awakening is actually a molecular energizing.
We come and rest and see the familiar ancient gods of the hearth.
Here, alone, by fate or by choice, I feel the stillness
that allows truth to surface.
Time alone in a place like this makes you appreciate
the time spent with others,
a magic place within a magic place.
The most precious thing that is hidden here is some part of yourself,
sleeping, dreaming, far from city strife.
Thank you to all that have left a piece of themselves
in this journal and in the others.
These individuals who have written here are my family.
I am so grateful for this spectacular and gentle place
and to Deetjen himself.

I don't know if it was fate, God, or some other thing
that "ended me up" in this place,
but they need to have more places like this all over the world.
The peacefulness and charm of a tiny room
with lots of windows and antique furniture . . . in solitude,
tender, like being in my own little sailboat.

ABOVE: The Fireplace Room now has a cozy, efficient, even-heating Norwegian wood-burning stove.
BELOW: Fireplace Room sign.

ABOVE: Petite Cuisine sign.
BELOW: Grandpa's Carriage Lamp Doorbell

What Really Matters

This journal rocks!

This sanctuary

This tiny room spoke to me right away.

The simple things of life, gentleness,

walls and furniture with a history.

Thank you for maintaining this gem

for us to realize what really matters: love.

The most comfortable feeling has washed over me.

I give myself this gift of The Petite Cuisine to bring in the New Year.

A classic Big Sur storm rages.

What a perfect nest!

You may even return to astonish yourself one day—with the clarity and beauty of your own thoughts, their desperate inspiration.

What's between us, between these pages, has a life of its own,

one more meaningful as a collection than as any one page.

The Teapot Journals

Petite Cuisine.

Silly name for a room.

I was shocked when I saw it: a closet with a bed . . .

and a sink . . . and windows.

Then I discovered the journals and the Teapot.

The room became magical and alive, just like Big Sur . . .

Thank you Lord, for little blessings like Deetjen's, and this little room.

This place is heaven—this journal, a touchstone.

We say things anonymously . . .

We come here again and again,

attributing healing and relief to this place . . .

the old buildings' sense of strength, surviving time—a place

where I feel protected.

Little did I realize that Petite Cuisine even existed.

What a great discovery!

This little room is symbolic of the magic,

and each of you who reads these words knows what I'm referring to.

Does Petite Cuisine make us feel safe in its solitude and spirit?

I strive to take this spirit with me.

The View Inside

(Consider: Do you realize how quiet one must be in a little room
to even find these journals and the teapot!)
This little room . . . the symbol of a cocoon . . . I leave as a butterfly.
Blessings to all who pass through this enchanted little room.
Thanks, Deetjen's, for keeping such a cozy and affordable little room
for us solitary wanderers.
There is something about the snugness of this room
that makes it difficult for me to be lonely.
This entry is being written because
next year, we'll want to see what we wrote last year.
I stumbled upon Deetjen's Big Sur Inn in the darkness.
I feel as though I have swum the beckoning sea of renewal,
wallowed through the clouds of my life.
I have read everything in the teapot and most of the journals.
I feel touched to share in this progression,
and moved by the richness and wisdom of those
who have passed before me here.
Thank you Deetjen's for a soul-restoring stay.
Thank you to the gentle spirits that abide in this room . . .
Thank you adorable cubbyhole.

Room for Inspiration

Strangers of the Future

It was like going back into my childhood
when I was safe and comforted . . . loved and protected.
It made everything simple again.
No need for extra stuff.
This room has character and history.
My heart swells with joy for the opportunity to turn my soul inside out
and share it with strangers of the future.
May all of us find our soul and our heart, spirit and path in this special place.
What soulful, beautiful, open, love-seeking, optimistic and loving people
one meets through the pages of this—and the companion journals.

In These Quarters

We are together in that we are alone.
We have come with our lives to this small room, in solitude—and found
in strangers, a community, a sharing—quiet and remarkably profound.
When we meet . . . by chance . . . will a recognition come?
And will we ask: "Was that you?"
I like to think Grandpa Deetjen knew his creation
would hold similar meaning
to at least some of his guests. Or rather, I'm confident that he did.
I started reading and the room got more and more filled with these stories,
emotions, and thoughts . . . It isn't like one of those anonymous hotel rooms
because there is so much life, such a soul in here.
I feel . . . somehow at home.

I fell to sleep after glimpsing the lives of all who came before me . . .
who left their hearts, souls, pains, joys, past sorrows, future dreams
and insights in the journals, safely tucked away in these quarters.
All of them passed through me
as if I were in the center of a universe of energy.
At once, all those who have been comforted by this bed
snapped through my most inner spirit.
The experience reeled me.
I journeyed to a place I never knew I had.

FACING: Castro Canyon Cabin.
ABOVE: Hayloft window.
BELOW: Reading Room exterior in the fall

Room for Inspiration

ABOVE: Looking toward the Fireplace Room deck.
BELOW: Journal entry.
FACING: Castro Creek, looking toward bridge and Creek House.

THE SEQUENCE ONCE AGAIN. DEETJEN CREATED LOVE NESTS, LOVE PATHS AND LOVE VIEWS! I SHALL PARTAKE AGAIN OF ALL THESE PLEASURES. THIS ROOM GAVE ME THE TIME AND SPACE TO KNOW THESE JOYS CAN RETURN.

Something New
This is the last evidence of paper in this little journal.
Our commonality and spiritual connectedness . . . binds us
eternally to each other . . . .
Reflect on the gift we've been granted . . . .
smiles of joy and tears of sorrow.
We give this book to Deetjen's and the Honeymoon Room
and all the people who come after us
to commemorate our love and marriage today.
We sat in the chair and read this book aloud to each other, read about the great
food and the beaches, the hikes, the wonderful views.

But I am so overwhelmingly happy in this room on a stormy, stormy night
with the hail pelting the roof, talking and laughing, giggling with,
and making love to my most wonderful, beautiful husband.
I could stay in this magical little room with the warm stove
and the funny mirror and the big magnificent bed forever.
It's the first time I've felt at home in America.
Thank God there's no television.

Settling in Van Gogh becomes more pleasurable
as we read excerpts from the guest book . . . .
Tears stream down our faces as we peer into other people's vignettes.
Tales of love touch deep parts of our soul.
The love we share is full, rich and growing.
This place will be the site for a celebration of new beginnings.

Journal of Local History

What we were moving was Henry Miller's old bathtub
that had been propped up on bricks and a fire built under it
to create a true hot tub facing the wonderful Pacific.
We dare ya! We DOUBLE DARE ya' to call (214) ***-**** and say
"Hey! Saw your entry at Deetjen's, ya'll!"
The peace here in Big Sur is so profound . . .
breathing beauty and tranquility into our city lungs.
1994: This return visit to the Antique Apartment is a kind of homecoming.
a remembrance of days in 1969 and a night in 1982 . . . .
Happily, gratefully, the Inn remains a constant,
a touchstone of who I've been, who I am, and quite possibly who I will be.
My grandmother, Edith O'Ryan (Edy of "Edy's Room")
lived here for more than ten years, sharing her life, and working,
and giving love to so many people (and animals!)
We used to spend Christmas here with her,
making homemade decorations for the tree.
I had a pet raccoon.
I would climb the Seven Dwarfs Trail all the way to the top.
And if we were lucky, Joan Baez would join us
at the big dining room table for dinner.
What memories!

ABOVE: Cinderella Shop sign and Lucky the black cat, Halloween 1965
RIGHT: Forty years later, the Reading Room interior with Fabio the cat.

The Last Best Place

We came here to affirm what is really important.
And we came here to learn how to make love again.
I don't think it was the mirror, but it was the images . . .
reflected in the journals that I greedily devoured—
much like I devoured my lover . . .

I've come to Big Sur, to this room, to escape the never-ending interruptions
of my regular workplace.
Nobody knows where I am.
I'm not sure I do.

We have found the perfect place—The Antique Apartment.
Over these two nights, we have fed the fire and fed our souls.
Who needs TV when there is so much entertainment in these journals?
I have never stayed in a place that felt so much like home.
Thank you Fireplace Room for the solitude you have afforded me.
Our room, this room, still smells like last night's fire.
The electricity is still out from the fantastic thunderstorm
that rumbled through Big Sur in the middle of the night.
The rain has ceased, but everything outside drips and patters,
and the air feels damp and clean.
This place is the last best place.

ABOVE LEFT: Honeymoon Room mirror and stove.
ABOVE: Creek House, looking upstream.

Room for Inspiration

The writer hopes you see yourself in these lines, if not literally, then in spirit, and if not here, then wishing you were. Henry Miller declared, "There is no light on earth which matches the inner light." The warmth of each room at the Inn, the embers of countless nights at every hearth and woodstove kindle that inner light. Nowhere can a traveler feel more at peace. The hand-hewn character and homemade feel there, the unexpected cozy corners, touched with antiques and tended lovingly over time, invite and comfort the spirit. Somewhere between the images of these rooms and this written cross-section of lives lies the serendipity that defines Deetjen's.

A GHOST STORY

In *Ghosts of the Big Sur Coast*, Randall Reinstedt shares the following recollection, leaving it up to the reader to determine just which innkeeper had this experience:

After passing Nepenthe and continuing down the grade, we come to the Henry Miller Memorial Library, located in a small house that was once owned by Miller's good friend, Emil White. Did you know that this famed writer (author of such books as *Tropic of Cancer* and *Tropic of Capricorn*, and my favorite, *Big Sur and the Oranges of Hieronymous Bosch*) was a Big Sur resident for many years? Miller lived in the area—mostly atop Partington Ridge—from the mid-1940s to the early 1960s.

Another bend or two brings us to a rustic coastal inn, a place that to many—at least in the early days—represented the essence of Big Sur. Nestled in a canyon, and blending with the redwoods and a brisk mountain stream, this roadside retreat had its beginning before Highway One was completed and today looks back on many years of memories.

Uppermost among these memories, at least for those who knew the inn in decades past, are the times shared with Papa—the man who created this magical place. Unfortunately, Papa passed away in 1972. However, even though the spirit behind this "spot that time forgot" no longer holds court at the long table inside the board-and-batten barn (where the restaurant is now located), both residents and visitors who have long been a part of this Big Sur experience have reported seeing and feeling his presence.

Dressed in his usual attire—complete with suspenders—Papa usually appeared only to those who he knew. In his own special way, he added a "difficult to describe" feeling of warmth and goodwill to the many other positive experiences that are shared by a select group of guests who have long frequented the inn. Most of these "regulars" have spent the night among the memorabilia in "Papa's room."

One incident not of the positive variety took place in Papa's room in the late 1970s. Even though it is the only happening of its kind that has ever been reported (at least to my knowledge), I find it of more than passing interest, in part because of the innkeeper's intuition even before the event took place. As he described to me when we chatted several years ago, early one afternoon when he was raking

leaves near Papa's room, he looked up to see a young couple being escorted to the cabin-like quarters. Upon glancing at the pair, the innkeeper (who had been one of Papa's most trusted friends) had a strange feeling of doubt about the couple and whether they were "right for the room." However, when they appeared happy and excited about their lodgings, he shrugged off his concern and continued with his chores.

As evening approached and the inn's cozy restaurant became crowded with guests and good cheer, the innkeeper acted as host to those who partook of the excellent food, the classical music, and the warmth of the facility's many fireplaces. Along about 9:30, as the evening began to mellow, the phone suddenly

FACING: Sign at sunset.
ABOVE: Grandpa's Room! Is it haunted? Read Randall Reinstedt's "Ghost Story" and decide for yourself.

Room for Inspiration

rang, its jarring tones spoiling the ambiance of the night. Upon answering the call, the innkeeper felt his original doubts come back to haunt him, as on the line was the man who has registered to stay in Papa's room. Calling from a second location, the troubled man said that he and his wife had left "in a hurry," and that they wouldn't be spending the night after all. In continuing, he reported that in their haste to get out of the room, they had left some of their belongings, which they would return for in the morning.

More than a little concerned about what had taken place, the innkeeper hurried across the yard to Papa's room. When he reached the cabin, he was both surprised and annoyed to find the lights on, the door open, and the couple's things scattered about.

Upon entering the room to turn the lights out, he was immediately aware of Papa's presence. Not only was the feeling of presence stronger than he had ever experienced it before, but he also sensed that Papa wanted to be left alone. With the message being very clear, the innkeeper excused himself, bade Papa good night, turned off the lights, and quietly closed the door.

Early the next morning, the couple returned for their belongings. Not only did they not mention what had taken place to drive them away, but they didn't even ask for their money back! Several years after the event, when the innkeeper shared this account with me, he still had difficulty explaining what it was about the couple that made him wonder if they were "right for the room." However, he did take satisfaction in knowing that whatever it was that had made him have doubts about the pair, it was obviously shared by his long departed friend—the grand old man who had built the inn.

With all other experiences of the supernatural kind having been of the positive variety, and with Papa posthumously approving of the way things were being run, all indications pointed to many more years of happiness and success for this "up the creek and under the redwoods" Big Sur retreat.

ABOVE: Rose hips against brick.
BELOW: Open Dawn to Dusk, but not always awake.
FACING: Hayloft steps.

DIVINELY SUPERFLUOUS BEAUTY

The storm-dances of gulls, the barking game of seals,
Over and under the ocean . . .
Divinely superfluous beauty
Rules the games, presides over destinies, makes trees grow
And hills tower, waves fall.
The incredible beauty of joy
Stars with fire the joining of lips, O let our loves too
Be joined, there is not a maiden
Burns and thirsts for love
More than my blood for you, by the shore of seals while the wings
Weave like a web in the air
Divinely superfluous beauty.

Julia Pfeiffer Burns State Park. Photo by Kodiak Greenwood.

five

HANDS

Inside a cave in a narrow canyon near Tassajara
The vault of rock is painted with hands,
A multitude of hands in the twilight, a cloud of men's palms, no more,
No other picture. There's no one to say
Whether the brown shy quiet people who are dead intended
Religion or magic, or made their tracings
In the idleness of art; but over the division of years these careful
Signs-manual are now like a sealed message
Saying: "Look: we also were human; we had hands, not paws. All hail
You people with the cleverer hands, our supplanters
In the beautiful country; enjoy her a season, her beauty, and come down
And be supplanted; for you also are human."

Feeding the Soul

"Music is the poetry of sound," Deetjen said at a December dinner in 1968. "It takes hold of the mind and twists it into following." Music has played an essential part of the dining experience at Deetjen's since the advent of electricity in Big Sur. "Music should be a part of each soul's development," Edgar Cayce wrote in 1957. He observed, "If you learn music, you'll learn most of what there is to know—unless it's something bad." One of Deetjen's literary mentors, Henry David Thoreau, wrote in his *Journal*, "When I hear music, I fear no danger. I am invulnerable. I see no foe. I am related to the earliest times and to the latest." Though Deetjen chose sophisticated music for his guests, the selections mysteriously complemented the primitive nature of the canyon, and satisfied a sensual primordial need, one that diners continue to appreciate today.

"WITHIN THESE WALLS"

Deetjen started the practice, now spread along the coast, of playing classical music in the Inn's restaurant during the morning and evening meal service. In his time, the day often started with Handel's *Water Music*, and moved through the Baroque era. In the afternoon, when the restaurant closed, Deetjen used to say softly that it was time to hear the composition, "'Silence,' by God." In the hush came the ash-muffled snapping of embers from the hearth, the euphony of dishes and utensils clinking from the kitchen—the peaceful between-meal respite from the restaurant bustle. Even when the music stops, something inside the Inn sings, as if the strains linger in the air.

In the Composer's Corner of the Family Room, above the old LPs and the new CD

FACING: Deetjen's Norwegian friend Mike Anderson carved this driftwood sculpture in 1965, calling it "Grandpa's Last Fling." Grandpa placed it in the window, where it has remained for forty years.
ABOVE, TOP: "Without music, life would be a mistake" Nietzsche.
ABOVE: Deetjen's Music Corner had assigned places for Grandpa's favorite composers. Though the Inn now has a CD changer, many of his chosen selections play throughout breakfast and dinner. Signs carved by Stokes Evans.

changer, hangs a plaque Stokes Evans made: "Without music, life would be a mistake." Friedrich Nietzsche's succinct words from *Twilight of the Idol* sum up the vital place the classics command at Big Sur Inn. The music corner holds records of all periods in custom-made bins. Composers with their own nameplates carved by Stokes Evans include Mozart, Bach, Beethoven, Chopin, Grieg, Vivaldi, Handel, and simply Baroque, where he kept Albinoni, Corelli, Tartini, Telemann, Pachelbel, and the Bach sons, among others. A slot for "Record Played" sits empty. These reminders of earlier days remain, though a new sound system sends the classics flowing evenly through each room in the restaurant. If the Fireplace Room of the restaurant feels like the heart of the Inn, the Family Room, with Deetjen's carved table and benches and music from the ages, is its soul.

Late morning music shifted seamlessly from Baroque to Classical, mostly ending breakfast or brunch chronologically with Haydn, Mozart, and sometimes with the Brazilian sensation of the day, Laurindo Almeida, playing classical guitar. Though the selections of today are less deliberate and less directed than under Deetjen, chamber music still helps provide the "Food with Character" that Big Sur Inn advertised in 1950. Guests brought Deetjen music from all over the world, and his orchestral order changed somewhat with each gift.

Dinners started with a brisk fanfare, often with a Maurice André trumpet voluntary, fresh from France. Perhaps it served as a call to arms for the staff. Depending on new musical acquisitions, the season—and the season of Deetjen's life—the musical selections

FACING: Old Big Sur Inn sign. Photo by Noel Douglas Walling.
LEFT: Some of Deetjen's stein collection, "One of the Largest in the West," their 1950 ad states.
BELOW: "Within these sacred portals, revenge and hate must cease. The souls of straying mortals in love will find release." Sign carved by Stokes Evans.

varied, but never the tone. He loved the purity of the lute, Segovia's guitar, the recorder and flute, the somber force and rapier-like strains of Tartini—the rapid cadence of Baroque in minor keys. Deetjen enjoyed telling tales about the escapades of various composers. In the circles he had traveled, he learned many entertaining stories about musicians. Virtuoso violinist and accomplished swordsman Guiseppi Tartini fathered several illegitimate children, escaped Rome disguised as a monk, and then married in secret. Tartini, Deetjen said, wrote his "Devil's Trill" after the devil came to him in a dream!

Somewhere in each evening came Johann Pachelbel's *Canon in D Minor*. Though he loved the melodic excitement of Vivaldi and dedicated a special bin to his works, he joked that many of his compositions seemed to say, "Vi-val-di, Vi-val-di, Vi-val-di!" Asked, in later years why he so seldom played his favorite composer, Beethoven, Deetjen replied, "You don't go to church every day of the week!"

At Christmas, he played a variety of Old World carols, but the most frequent holiday album heard was *Noël* by Joan Baez, especially Side 2, which began with Baez singing Franz Schubert's "Ave Maria" in German. Toward the end of his life, he played Norwegian spiritual songs, often humming or singing along, as though heeding a call from his estranged homeland.

Feeding the Soul

One selection seldom varied; Acts 2 and 3 of Mozart's *Magic Flute* was the LP played each evening. As former employee David Morrison recalls, "Sides 4, 5, and 6 of *The Magic Flute* played starting at 9:10 p.m. every evening." Next to the music corner, mounted above the double doors inside the Family Room, is a reminder of Deetjen's fascination with *The Magic Flute*, a Stokes-carved sign from one of Sarastro's arias in the opera reads:

Within these sacred portals, revenge and hate must cease.
The souls of straying mortals in love will find release.

Closer to the German aria (a piece that often moved Deetjen to sing along at dinner) is this translation:

Within these walls so holy where men by love do live,
No vengeance can lie hidden; We all sins do forgive.

This aria ended each day with what one might consider his prayer for the Inn.

ANTIQUE AMBIENCE

At Deetjen's Inn, every corner of the dining area invites you in. Every wall surrounds you with comfort. The restaurant's warmth speaks of simple shared pleasures, the kaleidoscopic play of light from the fireplace on ceiling and floor, the flicker of candlelight reflecting on fresh flowers, casting delicate changing shadows on each table. The charm of the Inn—its nostalgic delight, the way it enfolds the spirit—has captivated decades of visitors, transporting them to a milder, less complicated time.

The Inn elicits an appreciation felt in few places. Stay long enough and you hear the exclamations of returning guests, always moved, always amazed, always grateful.

"It hasn't changed. That's what's so wonderful. You go back to some places you love, and you can't even recognize them. But not here."

"See how you can see through some of the knotholes, the single-wall construction?

ABOVE: *Opus 27* by George De Groat, who rented the Top House from Grandpa. Kind permission of Bill De Groat.
BELOW: An enamored guest pauses to photograph the table setting and flowers.
FACING: Grandpa's Norwegian troll eyes keep watch over diners in the Fireplace Room of the Restaurant, as they have for 65 years.

That's just not done now. And it's really too bad it isn't. It's why this place is so unusual."

If over time a recording could be made of these heartfelt whispers, the sentiments spoken at the restaurant would resemble and echo those written in the room journals. The calm enchantment, the cordial and tranquil atmosphere, inspire a steady flow of return visitors ready to savor the restaurant's food and surroundings.

Deetjen indeed built something to outlast himself. What looks so elemental was so many years in the making. A lifetime, really. How extraordinary to have built a place cherished in the memories of so many! The cubbyholes, nooks, and shelves display treasures—Grandma Deetjen's antiques and Grandpa Deetjen's stein collection—and make every place a new focal point. It seems hard to be there and not be in love. Unimaginable, really. Guests take a love for the Inn with them when they leave, knowing that more awaits them when they return.

"STEERING" THE COFFEE

Coffee at the restaurant tastes superb. For one thing, the Inn selects a fine quality blend, but the water in Castro Canyon certainly contributes to the consistently delicious brew. In Deetjen's day, the morning coffee had special significance. If there were a Western counterpart to the Japanese tea ceremony, Deetjen's coffee ceremony would come close. The combined vacuum and drip reservoir required constant tending, a process every employee and many a guest can recall, though the details of their recollections vary slightly. It required one person to stir the grounds gently clockwise, then counterclockwise—using an ice teaspoon. It also required precise timing. All the boiled water from the coffee urn had to move into the upper filter before the five-minute process could begin.

Mimi Anderson Fain recalls that Deetjen said it should be "steered," and whether that was his Norwegian accent or some navigational reference, we will never know. He did not trust this procedure to just any new employee. He gave the impression that this was an honor granted to only a few. Even a trusted guest would seek the coffee ceremony post. Richard Levine, whose frequent visits to the Inn began at age 7 with his parents, Wally and Ilene, recalled that the technique involved a lifting of the pinky, and that the spoon should never touch the sides of the filter. Deetjen took such particular care because he liked strong coffee, and because not "steering" it would cause more grounds to stick to the side of the tall metal filter, not the sort of wastefulness anyone who had endured the Depression and the deprivation of rationed coffee during World War II would ever do! The result was a cup of coffee powerful enough to keep the traveler "alert, aware, and attentive" (Grandpa's edict) to the Mexican border and well beyond—or if headed north, to Washington State.

ANCHOVY PASTE

The Deetjen breakfast ritual had an equally rare aspect—more than one actually. Breakfast cook Bob De Ford would receive his order direct from Deetjen—in Norwegian! The orthography, *"De sama skolda vera, mit salt de vana."* A rough translation from Deetjen's Bergen dialect: "The same as before, with salt in the water" is DeFord's memory. Salt prevents broken eggs from leaking wastefully into the boiling water. He would have two soft-boiled eggs (3-1/2 minutes), toast—"Dundee marmalade was a must," recalled DeFord—Triskits, Nokkelost, or Gammelost cheese in a wooden tub, anchovy paste in a tube, and his ceremonial cup of potent coffee. The Gammelost, literally "old cheese," came with a demand by the storekeeper that it be fetched the day it arrived at the cheese shop so as not to contaminate the delicate aroma of other specialty cheeses. One always knew when the lid came off the Gammelost tub! Not to be forgotten was a box of Milk-Bones and a glass of milk, more than half of which Deetjen poured into a signed Royal Staffordshire soup bowl and placed it gingerly on the cement floor for whatever dog or dogs happened to have pawed open the side door. Best not address Deetjen before coffee and expect a civil answer.

If Grandpa's above bill o' fare fails to whet the appetite, the current breakfast menu will. Most guests would consider anchovy paste an acquired taste at best. It has never been on the menu, even in Deetjen's day. The hand-engraved, copper-on-wood menus of the '60s finally gave way to the colorful, hand-printed calligraphy variety used for many years. The old copper-and-wood menus had a slot to slide the menu into, framing each page with an engraved design. The current breakfast and dinner menus offer a wider meal selection, expeditiously generated by computer.

CHEF FOR THREE DECADES

Bill De Groat worked at the Inn for thirty years—from 1964 to 1994—nearly all that time as the dinner chef. De Groat's luscious Sunday-night Leg of Lamb Special always brought in locals and return guests from outside the area, as did menu items on the other six days. Antique dealer Bill Tangeman was one such regular Sunday diner at the Family Table. Dinner rarely started until Grandpa arrived. Sometimes the Family Table had ten people, sometimes just one, but Deetjen almost never ate dinner alone. Sculptor Jim Hunolt recalled, "Jeffers used to come down there and have a meal with him [Deetjen] on Sundays. Not every Sunday of course, but he did mention to me that he had been good friends with Robinson Jeffers." That was during the 1950s and earlier—years before either De Groat or Hunolt came to the Inn—but Hunolt was instrumental in arranging the bronze casting of Arch Garner's bust of Robinson Jeffers. Jeffers placed its twin terra-cotta image between granite boulders at Tor House in Carmel, considering it too severe a likeness.

To know Helmuth Deetjen was to encounter one revelation after another. For those who had the patience and took the time to listen, Deetjen provided recipes for life week

FACING, ABOVE: Rosalia Byrne and Ryan Webster stare back at Grandpa's impish knothole eyes.
FACING: Menu from the 1970s (with prices). Courtesy of Deetjen's, Inc.
LEFT: Menu and memorabilia. Courtesy of Ed Gardien.

after week. For some, Deetjen seemed solemn and humorless; for others, quite the opposite. Nowhere could you find a better dinner conversationalist with a keener wit. Many of his adages and mannerisms live on; others were lost over time. Not lost, however, are the delicious recipes that bring Deetjen's its repeat customers.

Bill De Groat came here more or less by a happy accident after his father, artist George De Groat, fell in love with the Inn one rainy night. Bill recalled his father's first encounter with Deetjen and the Inn: "He was cold and hungry, and the lights were on in the Restaurant. There was the fire going in the fireplace, and Bob and Mimi [DeFord and Anderson], with Deetjen at the head of the table. He sat down with them. Then he began staying there." Some time later, Deetjen offered to rent the Top House to De Groat.

As time passed, Bill began caretaking the place for his dad, and finally took over as evening chef after DeFord left the Inn. De Groat, Edith O'Ryan, and Stokes Evans remained Deetjen's most loyal, long-standing, and trusted employees. "I never missed a Saturday night for eighteen years," he related. Though De Groat remembers Deetjen as a demanding taskmaster ("It was his way or the highway!"), he also said, "He was the best person who ever ran the Inn. He was intelligent and sane. I admired Deetjen more than anybody there, but my mind is open to his foibles, too."

De Groat credits the many people who contributed to keeping the Inn and its Restaurant in the character the Deetjens envisioned. He recalls a series of chefs before him, most not staying long. Among them though, Liz Nichols stood out as an excellent chef. "Lizzy was very good. She'd been to the Cordon Bleu School in Paris," he said. Later, following De Groat, Peter Charles became chef for a couple of years. "Deetjen's gain, Ventana's loss" as one magazine article put it. De Groat hopes people realize that a succession of dedicated workers have kept Big Sur Inn running, and still do. He remarked on the current staff, many of whom have returned over the years and brought with them the remembered traditions the Deetjens established: "I was grateful for certain things, you know. We could always express ourselves there. If some customers abused us, Ed [Gardien] would back you up; and Deetjen didn't put up with people who weren't in control—slamming doors and stepping on dogs!"

Though occasional frustrations surfaced, those typical of dealing with the public and with an ever-changing staff in such an isolated area, De Groat had much to be thankful for during his long tenure. "I will always be grateful to Ed Gardien for letting me take my kids [Erik and Anya] to work when they were little. For years and years, I was able to take them. I'd get stools, and Ani would help me put the cloves in the hams. There were a lot of good things that happened there."

FACING: Fireplace Room at the Restaurant.
ABOVE: Antique plates, most from when the Deetjens ran the Inn.
BELOW: Front entrance to the Big Sur Inn Restaurant.

Feeding the Soul

De Groat also fondly recalled the late Bert Acker, the dishwasher employed at the Inn for seventeen years, as being great to work with. He credits him with saving the Restaurant when fire once threatened it.

RUSTIC ELEGANCE

Big Sur Inn manager Bruce Neeb takes particular pride in the menu and wine list. As his kitchen manager, Neeb hired the caring and cheerful Chef de Cuisine Jessica Cichowski and sous-chef Justin Robarge to maintain the Inn's tradition of superior cuisine. Their consistently delicious food preparation makes reservations a necessity on weekends and during the summer months. Both Cichowski and Robarge received their training in New England, and arrived at the Inn in 2000. The two come up with the daily specials, and take inventory, Robarge expedites service, and does much of the hands-on work. He helps maintain the rigorous tempo of the kitchen, and thus allows Cichowski's focus to remain on food preparation. Both chefs perform their tasks to the Inn's fifty-year-old cadence of classical music, enhancing both the dining experience and the spirit. While the Inn itself appears rustic, each table setting has a functional elegance. Because of Cichowski and Robarge's talent and teamwork, the menu creations consistently have both superb taste and an appetizing presentation. *Vive les Chefs!*

GRANDPA'S GRAVY LIST

The Inn never had a beer and wine license during Deetjen's life, but people brought their own bottles—though never to the family table. No license appears to have been required when the Deetjens served beer in the '40s and '50s. When Ed Gardien assumed the position of manager just a year after Deetjen's death, he took on the job of finally securing a permit to dispense both beverages legally. Over the next several years, Gardien developed

ABOVE: Big Sur Inn Restaurant sign through the trees.
BELOW: Spring wisteria in bloom, lovingly trained and tended by Odile Segal.
FACING, ABOVE: Bottles lined the Family Room windows some 40 years ago.
FACING, BELOW: Wine-buyer Bob Cosgrove selects his list from small growers.

an extensive wine list, one that caught the attention of a *Los Angeles Times* reporter. He called the Inn's wine list "the best in the state" at that time. The article brought in new customers, some for wine only. One of them, recalled Gardien, was Clint Eastwood. He also said David Packard enjoyed visits to the Inn's restaurant.

With apparent success, Gardien frequented the Napa, Sonoma, and Mendocino areas in search of varietals. No matter how diverse the collection stored in his small cellar, Gardien continued to refer to the wine list as "Grandpa's Gravy List," in deference to Deetjen and the days when he served Gallo's Paisano to trusted guests (poured surreptitiously into a heavy crockery coffee cup). Grandpa dubbed the prohibited substance *gravy*.

Today, longtime Big Sur resident Bob Cosgrove, wine-buyer for the restaurant, takes a path less traveled when making up the Deetjen's Wine List. His preference is for small family growers. "That's completely me," says Cosgrove about the decision to seek the goodness of small growers. Bruce Neeb says that these lesser known wines are often superior to brand names. These are "labels a lot of people don't recognize because they're mom-and-pop operations," Neeb said. Cosgrove prides himself on locating and procuring the best of these. His list boasts eighty-two labels, the most ever at Deetjen's. Wine salespeople come to the Inn, but Cosgrove also visits vintners.

Cosgrove also works as a host and a server at the Inn. From behind the old oak bar, he fields wine list calls between waiting on guests. Responding to a caller, he replies, "Okay, so send us three boxes. Your timing's perfect."

Deetjen's is fortunate indeed to have Cosgrove's expertise. He previously worked as wine-buyer at Ventana in Big Sur and at two Los Angeles-area restaurants, and came to the Inn in 1995. With such an extensive wine reserve, not all are noted but the list to the right shows "By the Glass" selections. Guests often thank the wine buyer for his expert choices.

By The Glass

APERITIFS
Lillet
Bodegas Dios Baco ~ Fino dry
Sherry
Kir
Kir Royale ~ Champagne
Cocktail

WINE
Whites
Gruet Brut
DeLorimier Sauvignon Blanc
Tolosa "No Oak" Chardonnay
River Ranch Chardonnay
Reds
Summerland Cabernet
Keltie Brook Pinot Noir
Cline Red Truck ~ Syrah blend
Dry Creek Merlot
Port & Dessert Wines
Graham's 10 year Tawny
Heitz Napa Port
Bonny Doon Vinde Glacier

BEER
Anchor Steam
Heineken
Kaliber Non-Alcohol

Feeding the Soul

ABOVE: The Family Room at Christmas.
FACING: Royal Staffordshire China: For decades, Deetjen's was the only inn in America using this pattern.

RECIPES FROM THE RESTAURANT

The most popular dishes from the restaurant and Chef Jessica Cichowski are published here for the first time for everyone to enjoy.

CHICKPEA SPREAD

This is served with homemade bread instead of butter.

2 (8 ounce) cans chickpeas, drained
2 teaspoons ground cumin
1 teaspoon ground cayenne
1 teaspoon salt
4 cloves garlic
3 or 4 fresh lemons, squeezed
1 to 2 cups oil

Combine chickpeas, spices, garlic, and lemon juice in a processor until well blended; slowly pour in oil till the spread is smooth, adding a little water if it seems too thick. Add more spice or lemon juice to your liking.

Makes 2 to 3 cups

CREAM OF ROASTED GARLIC AND TOMATO SOUP

This soup is a big hit with newcomers and regulars alike.

3 tablespoons olive oil
3 heads garlic, peeled
4 onions, sliced
2 cups red table wine
2 (16 ounce) cans roasted tomatoes, crushed
1 (16 ounce) can tomato juice
3 cups heavy cream
Salt and pepper to taste
Garnish, if desired: fresh basil, grated cheese

Heat olive oil in a large soup pot. Add garlic and cook until golden brown; add onions and cook until transparent. Add red wine, bring to a simmer, and reduce by half. Add tomatoes and juice; let simmer for 30 to 35 minutes.

Puree soup with a hand blender or a standard blender. Add heavy cream along with salt and pepper to taste. If desired, sprinkle with fresh basil or grated cheese before serving.

Serves 4

RED WINE–POACHED PEAR WITH BLUE CHEESE AND WALNUTS

This salad is an all-time favorite on the menu.

3 or 4 pears of your choice, halved and cored
1 bottle red wine, enough to cover pears
1 teaspoon cinnamon
1/2 cup brown sugar
2 cups blue cheese of your choice, crumbled
1 cup walnuts (or nuts of your choice), chopped
Mixed field greens
Balsamic Vinaigrette (see recipe on p. 98)

Preheat oven to 350 degrees.

Place pears in a saucepan and cover with a mixture of red wine, cinnamon, and sugar. Bring to a boil on stovetop and let simmer until pears are just tender. Remove pears from liquid and cool.

Mix blue cheese and nuts to form a 2-inch ball and place in the cored part of the pear. Place pears in the oven to let cheese mixture melt slightly. To serve, place pear half on a bed of greens and drizzle with Balsamic Vinaigrette.

Serves 4

ABOVE: Staffordshire variation: These were hand-signed, introduced by Barbara Blake, and in use at the inn for decades.
FACING: Back of Staffordshire dinnerware.

Balsamic Vinaigrette

1 cup balsamic vinegar
2 tablespoons Dijon mustard
2 cloves garlic
1 shallot, peeled
1 cup vegetable oil
1 cup olive oil
Salt and pepper to taste
Mint Sauce (recipe below)

Blend vinegar, mustard, garlic, and shallot in a food processor; slowly add oils and continue blending until smooth. Add salt and pepper to taste. Serve over Red Wine–Poached Pear with Blue Cheese and Walnuts.

Makes 3 cups

Honey Mustard–Encrusted Rack of Lamb

Tangy mustard paired with roasted lamb ensures this popular entrée remains a favorite among guests.

1 or 2 tablespoons honey
1/2 to 1 cup Dijon mustard
Rack of lamb, frenched (an 8-rib rack will serve 3 to 4 people)
Breadcrumbs, preferably panko (Japanese)

Preheat oven to 400 degrees.

Combine honey and mustard, spread over rack of lamb, and then cover in breadcrumbs. Set rack on a roasting pan and roast for 35 to 40 minutes, or until lamb is done. Let rest 15 minutes before serving with Mint Sauce.

Serves 2 to 4

Mint Sauce

This mint sauce has been served at Deetjens for a long time as an enhancement for the Honey Mustard–Encrusted Rack of Lamb.

1 cup white vinegar
1 cup powdered sugar
1 bunch fresh mint

Combine vinegar and sugar in a saucepan, bring to a boil, and then remove from heat. Add fresh mint to hot liquid and steep for 30 minutes. Strain and cool before serving.

Makes 1 to 2 cups

Parmesan Risotto

*This fresh combination of cheese and rice is the perfect side dish
to complement just about any entrée.*

1 medium onion, diced
2 teaspoons olive oil
1 1/2 cups aborio rice
2 cups white wine
8 cups boiling water or stock
1 cup grated Parmesan cheese
Salt to taste
Chopped parsley to garnish

In a saucepan, sauté onions in olive oil until translucent. Add rice and stir. Pour in wine and stir until wine is cooked away, approximately one minute. Slowly add boiling water or stock to the rice a cup or two at a time while continuing to stir. Keep adding liquid until rice is tender.

Before serving, stir in Parmesan cheese and salt to taste; sprinkle with chopped parsley.

Serves 2 to 3

Crème Brûlée

*Just when guests sit back and declare that they cannot eat one more bite,
this fabulous dessert convinces them they can.*

7 cups heavy cream
12 ounces granulated sugar
2 vanilla beans, halved lengthwise
24 egg yolks
2 tablespoons vanilla extract
Granulated sugar for topping

Preheat oven to 350 degrees.

Blend cream, sugar, and vanilla beans in a heavy-bottomed saucepan. Heat to a simmer, taking care not to boil the cream. Remove from heat and slowly whisk in the egg yolks and vanilla extract.

Fill oven-safe cups with mixture and bake in a water bath for 40 to 45 minutes. Let cups cool to room temperature, and then place in the refrigerator until cold.

Before serving, sprinkle tops of baked custard with sugar; melt sugar with a hand torch until it caramelizes and forms a classic crème brûlée burnt top.

Serves 6

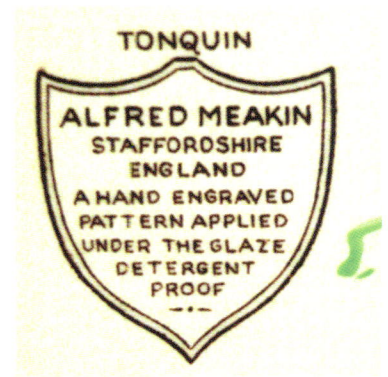

SERVICE BY LOCALS

The team of employees at Deetjen's Big Sur Inn displays dedication beyond the ordinary. Many stay for years. Others leave, find they miss the place, and return to work there years later. Still others just return repeatedly as customers. Fondness for the Inn seems nearly universal. Jim Hunolt, a Deetjen friend, former employee, and resident of Grandpa's Top House, eloquently expresses what so many feel:

> With little to start with, and in a country foreign to his birth, he constructed an empire, with the help of Helen and others, of course, that is an enduring beacon of Beauty and Refuge in a modern world that desperately needs both. No estimate could be made of the families, individuals, and couples that have discovered renewed hope and been nourished greatly by staying a day, or days, at his Big Sur Inn.

Currently, so many play a part at the Inn in bringing that "renewed hope" to travelers weary of seeing and feeling the same bleak sterility surround them at every vacation stop. Employees change over time, so acknowledgments remain inadequate. What does not change is the sensation of belonging that Inn guests feel. Not simply the Inn itself, but its people, make you feel at home.

The list of *Innkeepers*, while longer, and ever changing, has a common thread. Manager Bruce Neeb sees the need to keep the Inn's local flavor, and does so by employing a local staff. "They live on the coast, and can pop off directions," says Neeb. He wants to employ people with strong ties to the community. Neeb himself came to Big Sur in 1972 and established Earthfriends, a landscape design and installation company. He was manager of Esalen Institute and has served on the Big Sur Inn Preservation Foundation

The Family Table, hand-carved by Deetjen, with matching benches.

as a board member since 1991. Additionally, Neeb served on the Big Sur Land Use Advisory to the Monterey County Planning Commission, familiarizing himself with a variety of land use issues. Though he did not work directly for Deetjen, he has a sense of "the look and the feel of the place," as he puts it. His emphasis on encouraging local, longtime residents to stay on at the Inn ensures the continued integrity of Deetjen's that guests have come to expect.

THE JEFFERS CORNER

The Porch of the Inn, once a chilly, less desirable area to dine, has become a favorite space with many guests over the years. Historical photos surround the diners, and of particular interest in this room is the Jeffers Corner, which has Jeffers-related memorabilia as well as a bronze sculpture of Robinson Jeffers by Arch Garner. The following information by Jeff Garner, Arch Garner's son, recounts the impulsive origin of the work:

Jeffers Corner exterior.

> The portrait of Robinson Jeffers came about through the spur of the moment actions of Ward Ritchie, Gordon Newell, and Arch Garner. The occasion was the Occidental College Founders Day celebration of 1935, for which Occidental was celebrating its famous graduate, Jeffers, by giving him an honorary doctorate. Ritchie was a graduate of Oxy too, and Newell had attended there for most of his college study, having been a frat brother of Ritchie's. Ritchie and Newell were involved in the celebration, with displays of Ritchie's books and Newell's sculptures as part of the exhibition. Both were very enamored of Jeffers and his poetry, and saw him as a heroic example of the creative man.
>
> Ritchie hatched the plan that they should arrange for a portrait to be sculpted, and he and Newell immediately agreed that Garner should do the sculpting, as he was a portrait artist, and could work quickly. This was important because no prior arrangement had been made with Jeffers. In fact, he had no idea that the plan was underway. With only a phone call making the last minute request that he sit for a portrait, Jeffers agreed to sit for a short time. Packing Garner, Newell, clay, modeling stand, and a camera into his car, Ritchie drove them to the house where Jeffers and his wife Una were staying. The session went quickly, with Garner daubing the terra cotta onto the growing head, and then modeling Jeffers' likeness in the soft clay. Newell snapped photographs so that Garner would have a record from which to finish finer details. At some point in the sitting, Una remarked that Garner had gotten the characteristic flair of Jeffers nostrils, to which Jeffers responded by flaring them open widely.
>
> After the model was finished, several plaster copies were made. Two were apparently given to Jeffers, one in unfinished plaster that he incorporated into the masonry along the sash of a small window on the ocean side of the Tor House in Carmel. The other, a piece either of plaster with a faux bronze finish (as Garner often finished his portraits) or possibly cast in bronze, was at the Tor House for many years, until it went to a private collection somewhere in the Midwest. A photograph of it is still in the Tor House collection. Jeffers apparently didn't care for the portrait, at least he preferred the one

made of him by Jo Davidson several years before Garner's. It is easy to imagine why, as Davidson's is much more actively expressive, even joyous in its countenance, and somewhat smaller than life sized, making it lighthearted and playful looking. Garner's, typical of his ultra realistic, slightly larger than life style, is quite probably the more accurate likeness, but is rather severe by comparison. Jeffers was not entirely comfortable with the austere severity of character that was usually attributed to him as the result of the darkness of his poetry, and this might well have colored his appreciation of the work. An unfinished plaster copy is in the Special Collections archives at Occidental College, where it is sometimes displayed. A lacquered plaster copy was given by Garner to the city of Carmel's Sunset Center, and it has subsequently been given to the Tor House Foundation

A bronze copy was made for Deetjen's Big Sur Inn, where there is a "Jeffers Corner" in the dining room of the café. The bronze was taken from the copy at Sunset Center, the footwork being done by Jim Hunolt. Hunolt was a former employee of Deetjen's and a resident there. In the nineteen-sixties, he would begin sculpting under the tutelage of Newell at the Sculpture Center that Newell and Garner had founded on Cannery Row in Monterey. Hunolt had become Newell's star student, and a close friend from that time on.

A 1978 article in the Santa Barbara News Press shows a photograph of the work, indicating that it was being shown in an exhibition in the UCSB library's Special Collections, on the occasion of the donation of a private collection of Jeffers material. The article erroneously credits the work to Newell. The Special Collections department currently has no record of the work ever having been in their collection, so without further research, the ownership and location of that copy is unclear. I know of no other copies, although there may have been many more made, given the number of Jeffers fans in Ritchie's circle of friends and colleagues. I know of no copy having been in Ritchie's collection in his later years, although it seems likely that he would have had one, since it was his idea in the first place.

Without Jim Hunolt's sculpting knowledge, attention to detail, and, above all, the devotion to Deetjen and the Inn, the casting of this work would not have happened. Hunolt acted, as he put it, as "the medium that allowed the bust of Robinson Jeffers to become a part of Deetjen's." Hunolt recalled:

> Arch Garner, who became a very dear friend of mine while we were engaged in the epic experience that was the Monterey Sculpture Center on Cannery Row, gave me a plaster cast of his sculpture of Robinson Jeffers. . . . Sometime after Arch's death, it occurred to me that Grandpa might like to have a bronze casting of it as he had mentioned his friendship with Jeffers so very many times. I conferred with Gordon Newell about the appropriateness of making this offer to Deetjen considering the fact that Arch was no longer around. Gordon, who had been a life long friend of Arch's, was certain that Arch would have been honored to have this all transpire, so I showed the plaster piece to Grandpa and he loved it. I had the sculpture cast at a foundry in San Francisco, and Deetjen paid the casting fee. Stokes made the pedestal.

The sculpture brought as much warmth to that room as the woodstove Ed Gardien placed at its entrance. Jim Hunolt lived and worked as a sculptor at the Top House for ten years, though he only worked one summer, his first, for Grandpa. It would seem hard to imagine the Inn's restaurant without that distinct flash of inspiration, the contribution Hunolt brought to life.

> The whole experience of knowing Arch, what a dear soul he was, loving Jeffers' poetry, the conference with Gordon, which was so heartfelt, and my fondness for Grandpa, made the entire experience very benevolent and spiritually significant. And, of course, Stokes was honored to be a participant in this mini-epic event. . . . Arch, Jeffers, Grandpa, Gordon, and Stokes are now in the next dimension. I am the lone hold out of active participants, and I remember it all with extreme fondness.

Hunolt said he and Stokes used the event for many a toast, with gallons of red wine "on occasions of excess up at Top House," an observance that Innkeeper Emeritus Helmuth Deetjen would have savored.

FACING, ABOVE: The Jeffers Table in the Jeffers Corner on the Porch of the Restaurant surrounds the diners with Jeffers and Deetjen family memorabilia.
FACING, BELOW Catherine and Gibbs Smith enjoy a summer dinner on the Restaurant's Porch.
ABOVE: Outside the restaurant, Deetjen hung the couple's camping utensils on the batten board siding. Photo by Noel Douglas Walling

from TOR HOUSE

Come in the morning you will see white gulls
Weaving a dance over blue water, the wane of the moon
Their dance-companion, a ghost walking
By daylight, but wider and whiter than any bird in the world.
My ghost you needn't look for; it is probably
Here, but a dark one, deep in the granite, not dancing on wind
With the mad wings and the day moon.

LEFT: At sculptor Jim Hunolt's suggestion, Deetjen had Hunolt cast this Jeffers bust by Arch Garner at a foundry in San Francisco.

RIGHT: The terra-cotta match by Garner is nestled in an inaccessible wall at the Robinson Jeffers Tor House in Carmel. Occidental College (Jeffers, Arch Garner, and Gordon Newell's alma mater) has the other terra-cotta, conceived in 1935 when Jeffers received an honorary doctorate. Courtesy of Robinson Jeffers Tor House Foundation.

Sycamore Leaf in Coastal Stream. Photo by Kodiak Greenwood.

six

OCTOBER EVENING

Male-throated under the shallow sea-fog
Moaned a ship's horn quivering the shorelong granite.
Coyotes toward the valley made answer,
Their little wolf-pads in the dead grass by the stream
Wet with the young season's first rain,
Their jagged wail trespassing among the steep stars.
What stars? Aldebaran under the dove-leash
Pleiades. I thought, in an hour Orion will be risen,
Be glad for summer is dead and the sky
Turns over to darkness, good storms, few guests, glad rivers.

Deetjen on His Own

Getting to know Deetjen was difficult. Forgetting him, impossible. Everyone could agree on that, whether you loved him or wished you had never met him. He had a presence and made a powerful indelible impression. He changed lives. One could say the same of Mrs. Deetjen, though there are fewer left who knew her.

The Deetjens shared a love of the quieter months in Big Sur, though it meant less money coming in. They were somewhat reluctant innkeepers; having instead set out to leave behind the trappings of civilization, they found themselves, of sheer necessity, catering to it. That role did not come easy for Deetjen, who often discouraged guests by phone, saying when asked for directions that if people were meant to stay at the Inn, they would find it.

He shunned advertising, other than the ads placed at the behest of Barbara Blake. Once when a guest from United Airlines stayed at the Inn, he asked Deetjen for an interview. Deetjen liked him and gave a few comments. When the 1965 article and photos appeared in United's *Mainliner*, and the magazine made its way into each seat pocket in the fleet, Helmuth felt overwhelmed. "I didn't know so many people took airplanes," he said slowly. He said everything slowly. He stayed informed about current events by radio and newspaper, but having watched civilization develop at something of a distance, he had little idea that jet travel, still in its relative infancy, had become so pervasive. A quote from the article says that Deetjen loathes publicity, and that he agreed to pose "only on condition that the story will contain a clause that he doesn't want any more business, so would people please stay away from his Inn." To no one's surprise, the clause failed to deter visitors.

FACING: Deetjen takes the helm.
ABOVE, TOP: On his desk, Deetjen kept the happy Buddha, Hotei; in the background was a lovely Sumi painting of Helen.
BELOW: Helen Haight Deetjen at her desk in what is now Grandpa's Room, 1955. Helen Haight Deetjen.
Photograph by Brett Weston.
© The Brett Weston Archive.

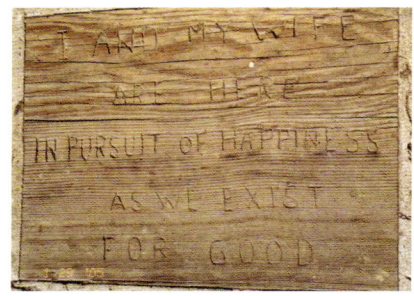

ABOVE: Bell from Ed Gardien! Frame by Stokes Evans.

ABOVE: Wood plaque: "I AND MY WIFE ARE HERE IN PURSUIT OF HAPPINESS AS WE EXIST FOR GOOD." Photo by Jane Sanders.

"I AND MY WIFE..."

At the front door, a foot-worn wooden floor plaque, embedded in concrete and barely legible, greets the restaurant visitor and states Helmuth and Helen's mission. "I AND MY WIFE ARE HERE IN PURSUIT OF HAPPINESS AS WE EXIST FOR GOOD." Those words leave no doubt that the Inn remained a labor of love throughout both their lives.

The year 1962, when Deetjen assumed full responsibility for the Inn, could not have been a worse time for him. It brought the deaths of his wife, his friend Johan Hagemeyer, and his friend and mentor Robinson Jeffers. The pressures of managing the Inn solo at the relatively advanced age of 69 took years for Deetjen to grow into, and it was never easy for him, by training or temperament, to adopt that role. It would be hard to imagine a more stressful decade for fate to cast Deetjen as sole innkeeper than the '60s. His physical condition had weakened; arthritis and his back tormented him.

After thirty years with Helen, twenty-five of them at the Inn, he no doubt missed hearing her lyrical summons, as Bob DeFord sings it,

"HELmuth. It's time to come HOME now."

"COMing, Helen," he'd sing back, and settle in for more conversation and another drink.

Later, and a half-note higher, would come the second call, "HELmuth, it's time to come HOME now."

So it would go, across the courtyard, until DeFord or another employee would make the slow evening shuffle, escorting him back to their quarters.

Helen managed. Helmuth built. She had complete control of the financial decisions regarding the Inn. She chose where they shopped and what they bought. She carried large amounts of cash on their town trips, though because of her weight and ill health, she sent others in to make purchases. Helen and Helmuth's interdependence had seen many twists and turns during the caretaking, courting, camping, marriage, and years of building. Losing his symbiotic relationship with her took its toll and disrupted the sense of stability he depended on. When Deetjen would talk of his "vife" at dinner, it was with a distant longing look. No matter to him that she outweighed him twice; it was what they accomplished together that counted. Yes, she ate too much and he drank too much. No one will ever know all the complex causes of those tendencies. Yet the labels people tend to lean on cannot define the Deetjens. They fit no known stereotypes. As individualists, few on the coast could match their rugged nature. They dared to carry out their dreams, and though not every one of them came true, most did. Thousands of people every year remain thankful for that without ever realizing the years of hardscrabble building it took to produce the refuge that is today's Big Sur Inn.

ABOVE, LEFT: **Helen's view from the Top Antique.**

CARRYING ON

Though Deetjen's capricious manner frequently perplexed and infuriated employees, numerous workers through the years remained devoted, if not to him, then to the Inn—his essence. After an argument with Grandpa, Ed Gardien once told him, "I don't like you, but I love the Inn." Later, Ed remarked, "Deetjen seemed satisfied with that." Because the Inn was an extension of Grandpa's persona, it made the remark less caustic.

The combined internal and external pressures Grandpa felt on his watch would have greatly vexed anyone. If aging itself were not a sufficient challenge, the decade's sudden cultural changes ran counter to the solid work ethic he valued, and left him unsettled. Throughout the country and along the coast, the beginnings of drug use surfaced and became rampant during his tenure. This change in the local and national lifestyle challenged his business. Deetjen needed strong control at a time when he was ill prepared, physically and psychologically, to embrace his new role. His control and coping mechanisms as a manager ranged from gentility to near tyranny. His workers saw far more of his unpredictable behavior than did his friends and guests, though no one had total immunity—including the rich and famous.

On more than one occasion, he would lash out with the swiftness and precision of a striking raptor. "Get her out of here," he would mutter to some employee, who then had the unenviable task of asking a well-known singer—whose music Grandpa loved, whose voice he said was angelic—to leave! No one seemed certain of the reason. Long hair, perhaps. For during that same time, Deetjen kept numerous signs instructing employees who to serve and who not to serve. One evening, a local but nationally known singer brought his own

Deetjen on His Own 111

Bob DeFord, Deetjen friend and confidant, worked seven years at the Inn in the 1960s, and Bettie Sue Walters worked briefly for Deetjen before his death in 1972. Both have vivid memories of their time with Grandpa. Sign by Stokes Evans.

fine wine to the family table for a dinner party. Deetjen demanded he leave the wine outside. At the time, the Inn had no beer and wine license. An uncomfortable argument ensued, and had the party not headed north to Ventana, he was about to have them ousted.

MORE "GRAVY"

Deetjen offered wine at the family table when he felt secure with the guests but never mentioned the word. He would ask if you would like "gravy"—the Deetjen code word for red wine. He served (and drank) so much gravy that Ernest and Julio Gallo sent him a personal letter of appreciation and several free gallons, plus some of their finer wines.

Deetjen, as well as his staff, closed their eyes to guests who brought their own wine, but at the family table, the only offering was Grandpa's gravy. An infraction, particularly if Deetjen saw it, could bring a fine or worse to the restaurant. Bettie Sue Walters recalled the genesis of the original wine list:

> Ed [Gardien] got the wine license when he took over, and started "Grandpa's Gravy List" with some house wines and carafes. He was very interested in wines. Ed built the first list. Back when Grandpa was alive, people would bring their own bottles. It was well known.

"STOKES!"

Deetjen did not run the Inn unassisted. His devoted staff outnumbered temporary summer help. Foremost among those loyal to the Inn and its owners was Stokes Evans. The name "Stokes!" would ring out across the canyon like a two-bell custodian's call at a school. Deetjen had a myriad of inflections he could put on that name, and it always meant business—a leak, a broken hinge, the need for firewood, wiring repair, a clogged culvert. If it had to do with maintenance, Stokes could fix it. His name was synonymous with "needs repair" and signaled everything from a true maintenance need to a state of mind Grandpa felt needed correction. He would say the name softly and indicate with a wink that he thought someone was not thinking straight, that maybe Stokes could repair the damage.

Stokes worked for Deetjen's for twenty years, devotedly maintaining the Inn through the deaths of both the Deetjens and the transitional times that followed. His love of the place came through in innumerable ways. He made signs and cabinets, framed photographs and paintings, built rock walls, and maintained the Inn as though he had built it. He had no idea how Deetjen valued his talents, admired his work, and depended on him. Though Deetjen let others know the admiration he had for his handyman, he seldom expressed that appreciation to Stokes himself. They shared a complex and cordial relationship, with Deetjen always keeping the upper hand. The Inn honored Stokes by having a cabin named for him. The building, now a rental, also housed his former workshop just across the bridge, near Castro Creek. Deetjen deeply valued Stokes for his hard work, his lengthy service, his love of the Inn, and his loyalty.

ABOVE: Stokes with dogs.
BELOW: Stokes Evans completes work on a rock retaining wall following a Big Sur storm. Due to Stokes' faithful service to the Inn and the Deetjens, management named a room for him.

Edith O'Ryan, Deetjen's accountant, loved all the Deetjen animals. She sits in front of the room now named in her honor, Edy's Room.

EDITH O'RYAN

Edith O'Ryan, Deetjen's accountant, came to the Inn following a dramatic 1956 rescue at sea from the sinking Stockholm steamer *Andrea Doria*. If she thought her land-based life would lack excitement, she came to the wrong place. No sooner had the Georgia native arrived in Big Sur than she encountered one of its well-known landslides. In 1957, O'Ryan looked off her Laffler Canyon deck the morning after a severe storm. A landslide took out Highway One to the north, and from where she stood she expected to see the river. Instead she could see a drop directly to the ocean. The slide had undermined the deck where she usually enjoyed her mornings—and where she was standing! Shortly after the road reopened, O'Ryan took up residence next to the Franklin Room at the Inn, and became an invaluable member of the Deetjen support system. Deetjen had complete respect for her. He called her his right hand, and if they argued, she won. O'Ryan made Deetjen's paperwork life possible. The staff loved her, especially Ed Gardien, a fellow Georgia-born transplant, and Bill De Groat. She loved bringing her granddaughter, Palmer, to the Inn for visits. Edie (or Edy) left her imprint on the Inn, and her former room carries her name and spirit—with photos taken during her years of indispensable service there.

If O'Ryan needed advice, that fell to Carmel "Cappy" Martin Jr., Deetjen's trusted attorney in Monterey. His diligence and creative thinking saved the Inn after Deetjen died. Of Martin, fellow Deetjen's Inc. board member Don McQueen says, "He was the only really super honest lawyer I've ever known. He went way beyond honest." Martin's scrupulous attention to detail on Deetjen's behalf, both before and after his death, continues to affect the Inn in positive ways.

BILL DE GROAT RECALLS DEETJEN

In 1980, just eight years after Deetjen's death, the Inn's soft-spoken chef, Bill De Groat, gave a taped interview of his vivid recollections of Deetjen and a sense of what it was like to work for him. De Groat said Deetjen was "always a very quiet man" who built the place not so much to make money as for other reasons. He saw the Inn as a "spiritual retreat." De Groat said:

> Deetjen studied philosophy when he was young.... He knew a lot of the famous people from the twentieth century. He liked to talk about them at the dinner table. I've never met a man who knew more about philosophy and comparative religions and history. He was just amazing. He was really clear-minded, very articulate. People often used to come down to stay and talk at the dinner table. He did enjoy his wine with dinner. All I can say is he was very well liked. Deetjen liked people, but never really got close to them.
>
> I used to walk him home. [The Inn] was a reflection of his inner life. It wasn't a commercial enterprise. He was a very complicated guy. He could often be brusque, and people who didn't know him would be turned off by that. He was an Old World person. He

Bill De Groat, chef for three decades, married his wife, Jill, at the Inn. Shown behind the couple, Ed Gardien and Faye Harrington.

was isolated here for so long he didn't keep up with modern American cultural developments. He didn't know about the social changes, especially that young people were going through. But that's one reason so many young people worked here. One of the things he thought about the Inn is that it was a place for young people to grow. They had to work very hard then and many people weren't used to working that hard. He commanded an Old World regime, but everybody that ever worked here got something out of it.

I wish I had known Mrs. Deetjen. She died a few years before I came, but all the old timers around here had nothing but good to say about her. She was very well respected.

We really worked hard in those days. There's no question it was much harder! Deetjen had what he called his Three A's: "Awareness, Alertness, and Attention," and we were here to learn those things. The way we worked then had nothing to do with schedules or being paid by the hour. It was like a privilege that he'd allow you to work here. You just were here at 7:30 or 8:00 in the morning and worked all day—with a two-hour break, if you were lucky....

People were happier then, even though they were working harder.... He was such a strong person he could motivate young people to give to the Inn, and that's actually the story of the Inn's success, is that not only Deetjen, but all the people that have worked here have given things, and it's sort of developed into what it is now. It's not a flashy place or anything. It is a living place that needs people relating to each other,

ABOVE: "So leave awhile the paw-marks on the front door, where I used to scratch to go out or in . . . ." from Robinson Jeffers "The House-Dog's Grave."

BELOW: Dogs were as welcome at the Inn as they were welcoming. The Van Gogh–gouged doors, sculpted by many paws, though now painted, still bear the marks of the Deetjen dog days.

rather than just a business or a shelter. Sometimes people just come in and they are just enthralled, and they look at things for hours, and they don't eat anything, they just look, and they leave refreshed.

It is one of the most unique places in the world. Not that the buildings are all that great, and I'm sure there are many older ones in the country, but there's something organic that fits into the landscape. It's unequalled. It's Big Sur. The buildings look as if they grew here. People that stop here often comment on that and how that feels. They are irreplaceable.

Following the interview in 1980, De Groat would go on to work another fourteen years at the Inn, living through what he considered its most turbulent years, from 1984 to 1994. He left the Inn after thirty years of employment there, and he left it a richer place. He was one of Grandpa's most trusted and loyal employees, so perhaps it is no coincidence that Deetjen died on De Groat's birthday.

GRANDPA WELCOMED PETS—OR PROVIDED THEM

Guests pulling into the property for the first time might assume they had arrived at an animal shelter instead of an inn. Visitors and employees who happened to be around during the '60s still laugh about the Dogs' Chorus, led by a dog named My-My. This daily event, usually right about 5:00 p.m., signaled the start of the news with Lowell Thomas. A dog food commercial would start her singing! Not howling. Not barking. Pure dog song. Those moments and at dinner were the only times she appeared without a green ball in her mouth; without it she was likely to bite anybody who approached. The ball served as both muzzle and pacifier, a Deetjen invention. Were he to choose between the comfort of one of his dogs and a guest (or employee), the dog always won!

Deetjen welcomed guest dogs. Take the Weimaraner named Bufo who has a storeroom named for him. Bufo's one-night stand came about when his road was evacuated during the Molera Fire in 1972. Grandpa directed an employee to place the hysterical animal (who had stayed before, but always in a guest room) in the storage room next to the Duck House. The severely claustrophobic Bufo lashed out at the man to protest his confinement. Grandpa had little to no respect for this person, so when the owner came to collect the refugee pooch, Grandpa informed her of the dog's health condition. "He's going to need a doctor," he said in a somewhat inebriated state. "He's going to need his stomach pumped!" She was puzzled by this until she saw the bandage covering the employee's arm, wrist to elbow. Only then did she understand Grandpa's stomach riddle. Stokes made a Bufo sign, and the guest Weimaraner took his place among the Inn's animal legends.

JAI RAM JAIL AND THE HOUSE OF CATS

Grandpa welcomed guest dogs but had the Jai Ram Jail for errant, endangered, or ill-mannered hounds. If a guest did not have a dog, he might just supply them with one. Until 1964, that would usually be Be-Be, a stalwart, mixed-breed trail companion. Be-Be vanished one day, but he is still the Inn's best-known dog after nearly fifty years. In the restaurant, you can ring one of Ed Gardien's brass bells that hang from a Stokes-framed 1964 photo and Stokes-carved nameplate: Be-Be. For years, beyond any hope of Be-Be's return, a sign read: "Ring for the Return of Be-Be." Doris Jolicoeur says she has not seen the sign in her twenty years at the Inn, but the sepia postcard of Be-Be resting in the middle of the road still sells, a symbolic hope for lost dogs everywhere.

Deetjen had Stokes build a "House of Cats," and he placed it behind the kitchen, nearest the leftovers—recycling, feline-style. Stokes used his prepositions with care, respectfully avoiding the label "Cat House." The kitty-call of the day, a two-note musical chant invented by Mimi Anderson Fain, would ring out in tune and on cue: "Key-OOP!" It ended on a higher note, and always beat out "Here, Kitty" for the cat-herding call. One of the many entrances in the House of Cats bore Mimi's name because of her rapport with the kitty crew. On the inside kitchen door, Deetjen wrote the names of generations of cats that had graced the Inn. No cat went without a name. One day some well-intentioned but oblivious cretin painted over all of them. What a delicate thin film is history! Deetjen was

ABOVE, TOP: Grandpa with My-My, his soprano pooch, who had the temperament of a prima donna, and needed her ubiquitous green ball to keep from biting people. The other Deetjen dogs, with one exception many years later, welcomed visitors, and were the Inn's emissaries.

ABOVE: The House of Cats, shown here in full operation, was located behind the kitchen, a feline recycling center.

Deetjen on His Own 117

a master at naming animals, especially cats, but the dog names had character as well. From Whiskey (the father) and Soda (the mother), he dubbed one of their sons "Hangover." However, the lengthy inventive list of hound dog handles is mostly lost.

Deetjen usually read after breakfast, just outside the restaurant's side entrance, with the five main dogs of the time: Shaggy, Puppy (pronounced ShaGEE, and PupPEE), Hangover, My-My, and the welcome stray Be-Be. Each dog's distinctive scratching on doorways sculpted them, making artistic clawed Van Gogh gouges—the adroit work of many a paw. Though now painted over, the dog-carved doors remain as a lovingly preserved tribute to each pooch and to the enduring love the Deetjens had for their pets.

HEEDING THE SIGNS

In his later years, aging and arthritis made Deetjen's personal room checks impossible. He relied on various rustically tasteful signs made by his friend Stokes, the most intriguing of them being the all-encompassing PLEASE HEED ALL SIGNS. The sign, now handsomely replaced by longtime maintenance manager Martin "Hubbs" Hubback, imparts something philosophical, even mystical—as if, in his seventies, Deetjen had found a succinct aphorism to sum up part of life itself. Other lesser-known signs dotted Deetjen's, some out of view of the guests. For example, Chef Bill De Groat recalled the one kept next to the pies: "All Beatniks and . . . [insert local name] . . . Refused Service." His signs ranged from general to highly specific.

FACING: Deetjen relied on many signs in his later years, none more than his "PLEASE HEED ALL SIGNS," shown in this double exposure.

ABOVE: Dogs waiting outside were a certain indication Deetjen was inside. His dogs rarely strayed far from him.

The various signs helped Deetjen feel in control of his domain, directing from a distance the actions of new and established employees. For the most part, they worked—not so much for the signs themselves, but by following them, one avoided incurring Deetjen's wrath.

Grandpa also had signs for himself. Over Deetjen's bed hung a sign just below his rifle, "Shoot Not in Fear or Anger." This left its use for food, self-defense, and mercy if an animal was beyond treatment. He came here intending to keep the harmony, not to break it. No one remembers Deetjen taking the rifle off the wall. In fact, when called to military duty in Norway, pacifist Deetjen refused to serve. Authorities jailed him, but he won a pardon from the King of Norway, so the story goes. According to Bob DeFord, "He claims the King of Norway came to his jail cell and talked to him" before his release.

The most powerful sign Deetjen had was never put in writing; it didn't need to be. Grandpa's best verbal attention-getter, "Yo Ho," would bring every employee in the place—the response always immediate and faster than when he would call out for Stokes!

THE WAY IT WAS

Cinematographer Robert Blaisdell captured Deetjen's sage remark in the video *Big Sur: The*

BELOW: Grandpa's Birthday Speech—November 14, 1967, framed by his friend and handyman Stokes, is reminiscent of Rilke, one of Deetjen's favorite German poets.

"So help me God . . . may I not in this time of my life stand upright here . . . may I not, so help me God, not say too much foolish. I have reached the time in my life that is compared to, in nature, with autumn. The leaves on the tree are no more green. They fall off the tree one by one like drips of rain from the eves of the roof . . . one by one they fall. The tree itself is not hurt in any way by what is going on. It is autumn in life, and the tree, very old, knows that after autumn comes winter with no leaf at all, but the tree knows it's still there. It knows more than that. It also knows that sometime, in God's time, there will be springtime and new leaves will be sprouting, and in eternity there will be new life."

Thank you,
Grandpa

(Grandpa Deetjen's Birthday Speech
Big Sur Inn, Big Sur, California,
November 14, 1967)

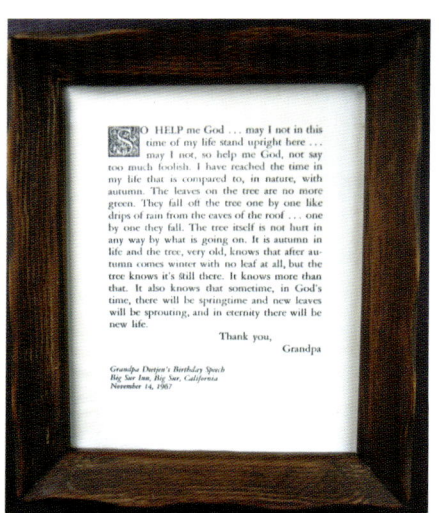

Way it Was (originally on 16mm film): "You have to have plenty to do if you want to live here, otherwise you go nuts." He filmed Deetjen for six hours to capture that and one other statement. Deetjen adages deserved to be recorded or written, but few were. Many who knew him expressed that regret. On sleep, Deetjen said, "If you miss the last hour before midnight, the damage is done." When a wildfire blazed above Big Sur, Deetjen observed, "There is no fire chief. The wind is the fire chief." Visitors who loved Deetjen would continually return, listening for the wisdom in his intriguing, often cryptic, remarks.

Deetjen's life spanned that rare epoch of human history, from horse carriage and hot air balloon days to jet travel and lunar exploration. In his personal life, he had moved from wealth to penury to self-made comfort. He walked through Europe and over the Old Coast Road and trails of Big Sur. He was comfortable communicating in three languages, and reading a fourth. He built his own dream world after filling the land by hand with a pickaxe. He built trails and homes. In terms of practical knowledge, it would be difficult to find an area of life he had not experienced. Because of the breadth of his expertise and his unique perspective, Deetjen made an engaging conversationalist—though appreciating him required persistence. An impatient dinner guest would leave the family table bewildered, never growing accustomed to Deetjen's accent, his peculiar way of phrasing things, or his long attention-getting pauses. To friends who returned—such as fellow countryman Mike Anderson (sculptor, mariner, and mystic), whose many works are at Big Sur Inn and the Stanton Center (Monterey's Maritime Museum), local antiques dealer Bill Tangeman, Dane George Keeleric, and fellow civil engineer Joe McClellan—as well as other repeat customers by the score, Grandpa did not disappoint.

RITUALS AND ROOM ROUNDS

The Deetjens ran a tight ship, and, when on his own, Grandpa did the same. They always attempted to hire people who would uphold standards they held dear. Time after time, the effort failed and Deetjen pointed the new-hire in the direction that he or she came from. When he made the rounds, Deetjen would flip up the bedspreads with his cane to check each bed. A properly made bed had clean-cut corners. Deetjen told DeFord, "There are seven ways to make a bed. There is the hospital way, the military way, the hotel way." The others DeFord could not recall, except for "*my* way, the *Deetjen* way." That method differed somewhat from "hospital corners," though very little. Former night manager Lu Dodson surmised that this rigorous practice stemmed from Mrs. Deetjen's background as a nurse. One important detail: Sheets and blankets should completely cover the shoulders. At that time, most rooms did not have heat, except those with a fireplace and the Franklin Room with its Franklin stove, so the Deetjens insisted on that bed-making detail for the comfort of the guests.

LEFT: Grandpa posed at his Dutch doors at Christmas in 1968 with the children of a Fairfield family—and Puppy on the buckboard wagon seat.

BELOW: Grandpa just informed Minnie Robertson that the redwood she intended to transplant is a fern. With his help, she planted a real redwood between apartment buildings in Sherman Oaks, California. Though both she and Grandpa are gone, the four-story tall redwood still grows there to the delight of tens of thousands of birds over the years.

BELOW, BOTTOM: If you celebrated your birthday at the Inn, and Deetjen learned of it, he always presented you with a special gift. Troubadour poet Ric Masten recalled receiving it. A silver dollar!

DEETJEN THE IRASCIBLE

Deetjen's passionate, impulsive, driven character made him completely impatient with indolence in any form. Work was his passion and it was what he best understood. Once he was unable to work and could only oversee it, he became a boss with exceedingly high expectations. Don McQueen said that Deetjen was wonderful to work for and that he gave clear directions, but that was when he was young, strong, able, and working alongside the people he hired. Deetjen valued intellectual companionship throughout his life, but as he grew older, he valued labor and loyalty every bit as much—perhaps more. The less physically capable he became, the more demanding he became of others.

Sculptor Jim Hunolt lived and worked in Deetjen's Top House for eight years. While he personally had a good relationship with Deetjen, he observed others who were less fortunate, and he found that dichotomy disturbing. He relates some of those feelings:

> There is no mistaking the fondness with which Grandpa is remembered today. This is evident, and extremely so, in the journals and written remembrances expressed so elegantly by those who had encounters with him years ago. These are precious, and he was able somehow to implant indelible impressions that affected, and even altered, many lives in incredibly positive ways.
>
> By 1964, when I met him first he had achieved all the basic goals he had set for himself. The Inn was built and successful. Money was no longer a problem, and to prove it he carried a humongous roll of bills with him at all times. The aura and routine of the Inn's daily operations were well established and he was surrounded by a staff of employees who considered themselves blessed to be living and working at Grandpa Deetjen's. He had entered a golden period of his life and he was well aware of it. . . .
>
> There really is no summation possible, no simple description available. He was the

From his captain's chair at dinner, the playful Deetjen purposely disheveled his hair and posed as Beethoven. On the photo, he wrote "Deethoven."

most serious enigma. He had a very dark side, yes. But his smile, the twinkle in his eye, the well chosen words, the depth of his perception, his ability to create enduring beauty that is having an incredibly positive legacy, and his amazing kindness to me are what I ultimately remember.

No one could feel comfortable with Deetjen when he chose to fire someone in a public manner, close the restaurant without warning, or in some other way display a side of his character he neither controlled nor understood. Deetjen had his demons, and he periodically unleashed them. Most who worked for him forgave those outbursts and awaited the return of his otherwise jovial disposition. Deetjen forgave or not, according to some inner accounting system. What that was, no one knew, but loyalty or the lack of it had everything to do with resetting his equilibrium.

PLAYFUL NATURE

Although his outbursts were famous, Deetjen possessed a fine sense of humor. He had a keen wit, and his quick mind would turn out memorable phrases, usually at dinner surrounded by friends. He played with words, enjoyed being silly at times, and loved formulating riddles. Deetjen took pleasure in confounding dinner guests as well as employees with riddles. Once at dinner, he kept everyone at the family table in suspense for most of the dinner hour with the comment, "I have discovered that the pathway to hell begins in this room." Guests offered several interpretations. When those went nowhere and Deetjen saw the sun setting, he steadily gazed shoulder-level out the window, apparently at one pane. Sure enough, one and only one pane glistened. The other forty-seven had a sooty interior and a spotty exterior; the window-washing task apparently was too daunting for the hired hand to complete. The road to hell is paved with good intentions. He could build a riddle out of any cliché. It might be days, or never, before someone understood his more enigmatic offerings.

Grandpa's ardent love of music also had its playful aspects, and as a young man, he had had some musical training. On exceedingly rare afternoons, Deetjen played a strangely pleasing piano—fierce and heavy-handed chords, a Norse pounding. The style fell somewhere between serious and jocular, but the performance clearly indicated that he once played before arthritis claimed his dexterity.

A SENSE OF PLACE

As Deetjen told Jim Hunolt, "You don't need to travel. You just find your place and do a good thing there, and the world will come to you." Grandpa came to feel no real need to travel farther than Carmel or Monterey. It was similar to the lion sculptures in front of the New York Public Library, where the tale states that if you stand long enough, you will see everyone you know. Deetjen said he felt that if he stayed at the Inn, he would eventually encounter everyone he wanted to meet. Some brought him delight, such as an all-day encounter with Jiddu Krishnamurti, who watched Deetjen intently, observing with particular fascination as he drilled holes with an old-fashioned brace and bit. He had never seen one, and as they talked, he asked Deetjen to demonstrate its use repeatedly. Then he tried, with wide circular motions, to use the tool, a story Grandpa loved sharing. Bob DeFord does his best Deetjen impersonation with this tale.

Not all guests are as welcome as Krishnamurti. For some travelers, Deetjen had little tolerance and no difficulty expressing distaste if he felt it. After all, hadn't this been his home first, before the visitor invasion became a livelihood? Perhaps because Deetjen considered this his home first and an Inn second, he had little tolerance for misdeeds within its walls. If there was to be a spate of bad behavior on his part, he may have had his reasons. As Hunolt reminds us, "Grandpa had a very stringent, dark, harsh side to him—that kept our attention." Deetjen did hire some workers who needed more than a little monitoring. His flare-ups, though short-lived, helped maintain what Deetjen liked to refer to as "ordered chaos." To stay at his Inn as guest or worker required one's finest behavior.

Steve Allen loved dining with Deetjen, and mentioned the Inn in one of his books. Hollywood stars of all ages found the Inn a refuge from publicity, a place where they could

Here, Grandpa poses in a red wig, sporting a cowbell. His door sign reads, "Mean Dogs;" but he wrote, "Mean dogs can also love. Helmuth Deetjen."

shed the stress of their own notoriety. Employees treated celebrities well but did not appear to cater to them more than they did other guests. Deetjen, who was once interested in Hollywood, now found that by staying still, Hollywood had come to him.

Deetjen had chosen this publicly cloistered life, but he saw the world and the control he had over his part of it slipping from his grasp. In the end, though definitions of the metaphysical fail miserably, Deetjen came closest to being a Christian mystic, judging from his discussions with confidants. Yet, every religion and philosophy he studied, he found worthwhile. He considered his highest purpose his work ethic—simply the way he lived his life. He identified with Kierkegaard and Christian existentialists. Deetjen's esoteric eclectic choices defy classification. Until his death, he remained a man who was both learning and teaching. Asked if he knew Deetjen, Big Sur poet Eric Barker questioned, "Did anyone know Deetjen?" Perhaps the answer to Barker's question is, "Only those who tried." Even of those who did, no one person can tell the Deetjen story.

Deetjen knew his death was eminent several weeks before he died. In a dream, he said he experienced the most angelic music he had ever heard. Asked if it was as beautiful as "Ode to Joy," Deetjen beamed, "It was better even than Beethoven!" Two days before he went to the hospital, the children from Captain Cooper School had planned a field trip, maps already in hand, up to the Seven Dwarfs' Homes along Ed Gardien's newly cut trail. When making arrangements for the excursion, Deetjen asked the teacher, "Will that be before the bulldozer, or after?" While many people know or sense their own demise, Deetjen did so with no dread whatever. He kept his sense of humor and riddle-making merriment to the end, and welcomed the celestial music, calling it "A Symphony of Angels."

Though Deetjen sought simplicity, he was a man of great complexity and contradiction, a charismatic figure who found his greatest peace in his personal brand of mysticism, the world's finest music and literature, the exhilaration he experienced in nature, the love and comfort of his pets, and the magnificent Inn he built with his wife. So much about Deetjen remains unknown. Its discovery would require another lifetime and far more translations from Norwegian, German, and possibly French—if any documents still exist. With his peers dead, many unique recollections remain buried as well. Deetjen remained deeply rooted in both reality and metaphysics, and those roots served humanity well.

The books Deejten left partially read were large-print paperback books. On a wooden shelf near his chair and his favorite blue-and-white antique lamp, he left *Love's Body* by Norman O. Brown, a book on humanity's condition—its slow drifting from a natural, intuitive, innocent state of being. Beneath it lay *The Pleasantries of the Incredible Mulla Nasrudin* by Idries Shah, an Afghan writer, and a third larger-print book folded open to

FACING: Deetjen collects the mail left by longtime mail carrier, Ed Culver—who also transported an occasional celebrity guest, Sue Lyon and others, when he left the mail. Deetjen liked the musical mailman, who doubled as a double bass player for a local symphony orchestra. Robinson Jeffers even rode down the coast with Culver.

LEFT: Grandpa, his yellow crock cup of strong coffee in hand, pauses to greet Lama, so named after Tibetan monks, not the animal.

BELOW: Helen and Helmuth's combined ashes are deep in the redwoods of Castro Canyon.

his place. Deetjen nourished his intense lengthy interest in Eastern and Western thought until the end of his life.

"AS WE EXIST FOR GOOD"

When Helmuth died, ten years and twenty days after Helen, her ashes, which had been buried in the canyon at a fork in the road, were unearthed and combined in an urn with his. Now buried together, deeper in the woods, the Deetjens have become part of the canyon they so loved.

I AND MY WIFE
ARE HERE
IN PURSUIT OF HAPPINESS
AS WE EXIST
FOR GOOD
Helmuth Deetjen: November 14, 1892—October 28, 1972
Helen Haight Deetjen: October 22, 1889—October 8, 1962

NOVEMBER SURF

Some lucky day each November great waves awake and are drawn
Like smoking mountains bright from the west
And come and cover the cliff with white violent cleanness: then suddenly
The old granite forgets half a year's filth:
The orange-peel, egg-shells, papers, pieces of clothing, the clots
Of dung in corners of the rock, and used
Sheaths that make light love safe in the evenings: all the droppings
    of the summer
Idlers washed off in a winter ecstasy:
I think this cumbered continent envies its cliff then. . . . But all seasons
The earth, in her childlike prophetic sleep,
Keeps dreaming of the bath of a storm that prepares up the long coast
Of the future to scour more than her sea-lines:
The cities gone down, the people fewer and the hawks more numerous,
The rivers mouth to source pure; when the two-footed
Mammal, being someways one of the nobler animals, regains
The dignity of room, the value of rareness.

Headlands and Storm Surge. Photo by Kodiak Greenwood.

Boulders in Streambed. Photo by Kodiak Greenwood.

seven

SIGN-POST

Civilized, crying how to be human again: this will tell you how.
Turn outward, love things, not men, turn right away from humanity,
Let that doll lie. Consider if you like how the lilies grow,
Lean on the silent rock until you feel its divinity
Make your veins cold, look at the silent stars, let your eyes
Climb the great ladder out of the pit of yourself and man.
Things are so beautiful, your love will follow your eyes;
Things are the God, you will love God, and not in vain,
For what we love, we grow to it, we share its nature. At length
You will look back along the stars' rays and see that even
The poor doll humanity has a place under heaven.
Its qualities repair their mosaic around you, the chips of strength
And sickness; but now you are free, even to become human,
But born of the rock and the air, not of a woman.

Friends of the Inn

T he Inn, its canyon, and the coast that is home to both—all of it speaks from some elemental source of energy. The newness of the land, the way it has risen suddenly and plunged, the wavelike look of it, the way it regenerates and grows, inspires us, touches a place in the human spirit where the ability to worship is born. The Big Sur coast, in fact the coast of the North and South American continents, tears at the soul and begs to be loved like a newborn pulled wet and glistening from the sea. Its quakes and storms, fires and mudslides, floods and tsunamis, from Alaska to Cape Horn, insure its near-eternal newness, thus allowing humanity to continue discovering a pristine place on earth—and in our own hearts as well.

VOICES, LETTERS, AND IMAGES

Some of those hearts speak throughout the pages of this book. Their voices marvel at the delicacy and solidity of the Inn and its surroundings, the inherent purity and regenerative power of both. To give voice and face to them all can no more happen than one can turn over every rock in a streambed. Still, the kinship of people who touched the Inn, and were touched by it—those observations need expression. The sentiments here no doubt echo those of the many who would wish to pay homage to Helen, Helmuth, or Big Sur Inn. From the pioneering spirit of the Deetjens to the poetic searching of their supplanters, the passion of each journey creates its own unique shape and purpose, and continues weaving the complex design of the Inn's tapestry. The Big Sur coast has a reputation of attracting those who live life on the edge, but as with every pattern in every fabric, the patterns of society must also be woven from the edge. To the faithful who stay for hours, or for decades, Deetjen's represents an archetype for change.

FACING: David Morrison worked two years at the Inn with Deetjen. He now makes his home in Oregon.
ABOVE, TOP: Mimi Anderson and Deetjen in the restaurant's Fireplace Room.
ABOVE: Eric Schandall has vivid recollections of his years at the Inn. His daughter was born next to Grandpa's Room. When he came to tell Grandpa the exciting news, Deetjen had only two words to say: "Educate her!"

Over the years, people who came to the Inn by chance have been drawn to remain or return. For each, whether visitor or worker, the Inn fulfilled a need, the end of longing, the beginning of belonging—like the recognition of an old friend, a homecoming. Limiting these stories to so few, while disappointing, is a necessity—one that will surely generate a continuity of future tales. So many workers have heartwarming and frustrating tales of their service at the Inn. A full accounting is impossible.

May these few vignettes, facets in a gemstone, offer flashes of insight and inspiration. As you read these brief experiences about life at Big Sur Inn, it becomes clear that Deetjen's is more about *place* than about any *one place*—about finding a place inside, something you keep with you, a personal renaissance. These individuals live diverse lives away from the Inn, but carry its essence in thoughts. They return when they can.

A HEALING PLACE

Jean Widaman fell in love with the poetry of Robinson Jeffers as a student at Occidental College. She set about an attempt to visit, insofar as possible, the setting of each of his poems on the Big Sur Coast, a passion that nearly cost her her life, and found her clinging to a steep slippery cliffside at one such location. Her first encounter with the Inn may not have been quite so dramatic, but it left as deep an impression and changed the focus of her pilgrimage.

Widaman remembers the big cluster of Shasta daisies, the wooden sculpture of the unicorn, the old green candleholder above the restaurant's fireplace, and the Handel flute sonatas. "Years later, I came to be playing those," she said. Now an accomplished musician, she remembers the enchantment of hearing Mozart's *Magic Flute* every night at the Inn.

"My first feeling was that I felt that this was really home," Widaman said. She camped in the canyon a couple of nights before landing a job and an upstairs apartment. She thought of Top Piano (now the office), with its ocean-view window, as prime staff housing. Not surprisingly, Top Piano was situated just above the dining room piano. The room had been the Deetjens first home—above the Workshop and Antique store, both of which became the Restaurant. In Widaman's two and a half years at the Inn, she said, "I saw Deetjen as an authority figure, a very big figure in my life." When talking about the Inn with someone else who knows it, she observes, "All of a sudden, you have a frame of reference."

"Grandpa came there and he built a stage, and the people came along and played the parts. They chose the role they needed to act out," said Widaman. She felt that many of these needs came from family issues, and that the Inn gave those who came there a chance to resolve problems. Widaman thinks of the Inn as "a healing place."

FACING: Cecil Brunner rose.
LEFT: New England–trained chef Jessica Cichowski and sous-chef Jason Robarge make the perfect mix in the Deetjen kitchen. Try the recipes in chapter five!

COSMIC COFFEE

Jim Hunolt's association with the Inn started in 1964 and has never ended. He set out to see the world, and like Deetjen in some ways, the world came to him instead, through his talents as a sculptor. When in Big Sur, Hunolt has breakfast at the Inn every morning. His feelings for Deetjen remain deeply conflicted, but he says: "Grandpa always, with one exception, treated me very well. Why I don't know, but it was as if we entered into an unspoken agreement that we established the first day we met. From the beginning, we had a mutual friendship that endured solidly until his death." He recalls that first summer in 1964:

> Something about the ambience made it feel so very warm and a little like a fairy tale. . . . I asked if there was some coffee. The old man said, "Nooooo . . . let's make some." . . . He asked me if I knew the only way to make proper coffee. I told him I didn't. He gave me this kind yet stern look. His eyes were doing all the talking. The secret is in the stirring and the little finger is what he told me. . . . The stirring motion is always circular. . . . The little finger must be up! No good coffee is ever made any other way! Proper coffee is only made using this technique. It is a mystery, alchemy in its finest hour.
>
> So began a conversation about coffee, just the two of us in this silent antique room, just talking about coffee. I loved it. He loved it. As we talked, my impression of him began to expand. At first he had seemed just to be a simple old country man, a little stooped, spoke a bit odd, kind of sloppily dressed in jeans and a plaid shirt. I soon

began to realize he was much more, and I mean in a sort of Cosmic sense. His language had a profundity to it, and he was able to imply a great deal while saying very little. Always in his eyes was a sparkle of humor, and it became clear to me that I was getting some kind of rare education between the words, the glances, the slight gestures. I began to get the idea that more was spoken than I could understand. . . .

My three day agreement with Grandpa Deetjen to make coffee and tend to guests at the bar in the restaurant stretched into weeks and finally into a full summer commitment. It opened my eyes to a portion of life I had not experienced: a free flowing, slightly sacred shared environment with one path, Grandpa's Way.

Grandpa's Way. On this one spot of our planet was revealed the teaching of Inn Management and Deportment as conceived of and executed by Helmuth Deetjen. We accepted this arrangement as an implied agreement of employment, and happily. In the summer of 1964, at least to the 9 or 10 of us that were in service at the Big Sur Inn, this was the Center of the Universe.

We had a Guru. He was benevolent and terrifying. We had teachings to learn and adhere to. Grandpa's do's and don't's. Some of these we were sure of, others changed seemingly at Grandpa's discretion or his mood. This uncertainty concerning procedures created an inherent sense of tension, or stress, which served to heighten our attention to details. This allowed, or forced, us into Grandpa's conception of blissful existence: Awareness!

No one knows what is going to happen next in life. This is especially true if you have a plan. . . . Four hours into my trip, on the first day, my expedition around America ended. Without even knowing it, I had reached my goal, or maybe my goal had simply reached me.

Before Hunolt, Peter Melchior lived in the Top House from the mid-fifties until 1972. "He saw Grandpa Deetjen as a teacher," said his wife Susan Melchior. Melchior studied at Esalen Institute with Dr. Ida K. Rolf before joining her organization in Boulder, Colorado, to become a founding faculty member of the Guild for Structural Integration.

BELOW: Reception for Bill and Jill De Groat, following their wedding ceremony in the Enchanted Room.
BELOW, RIGHT: Wedding reception for Ric and Patty Villa.

The Enchanted Room

I know a place
where heavy forest thins
a clearing
in the canyon's depth

There is a tree
fallen
long ago
full ten feet
through
the stump it left as altar
for this place
and I was told when I was young
that this would be the place where men
(real men—we are but shadows yet)
who will show forth splendor
in the simplest act
will meet
to form a lasting peace

A treaty will be signed here
which will not
be lightly taken
nor broken as before

This is what I have heard.
What I know is
this place sings to my soul
for I grew

here and was formed and re-formed
into what
I (for better of worse)
now am.
The heart of creation beats
in this canyon and a choir
sings
in the passage of the creek
which gives it life.

I slept in this place
every night
for a season
years ago.

When I walked away I carried
with me
wherever I went
the song I heard those voices sing

Once
I believed
I left much here
but it was not so much
what I left . . .

I did take much away
and must repay with my life
the debt I carry.

Peter Melchior
Big Sur, California, April 1966

Wedding of Ed and Kuniyo Gardien in the Enchanted Room.

UNDER CONSTRUCTION . . .

"It's a spiritual place; it's a temple," Ed Gardien observed when he still managed the Inn. "I can never put into words my feelings about the Inn. It came out in how I ran it." His association with the Inn spanned two decades. Bob DeFord remembers the day Ed Gardien rode up to the Inn on his bicycle. "He fit right in, of course," said DeFord. In a 2005 interview, the lanky Gardien recalled his first encounter with Deetjen.

> The first thing he said to me, when I rode up on my bicycle—I was coming from the North and I saw Mr. Deetjen standing in a place almost in the highway, right by the bridge. It was like he was waiting for something. I never saw him standing there again.

It was almost as if he was waiting for me. Deetjen was a mystic. He must have perceived me coming. That's the impression I got. Of course I was aware of who he was, but out of respect to him, I said, "Are you Mr. Deetjen?" And he looked at me for a long, *long* time. You know how he'd act. And then I didn't know what to say, so I just sort of stood there. Finally, he said, "The dwarfs have been looking for *you*."

Trail-blazer Deetjen envisioned a short trail to the dwarf homes, as he referred to seven of the fire-hollowed redwood stumps in the canyon; but his trail-cutting days had ended. Gardien, like so many who had merely paused on a lark, stopped his bicycle touring and began his varied association with the Inn. He took on the task of trail-building with his characteristic vigor, and completed the project in nine days, posting a Deetjen-worded sign: "Under construction: Trail to the Castle of Dreams Come True." Ed recalled, "Grandpa walked as far as where the little bend is, and he pointed out where he wanted the houses built." He said Deetjen told him he could take it from there. "The dwarfs will take you in hand," said Deetjen, who nicknamed his tall eighth dwarf *Stretched*, saying he was once a dwarf that had been stretched!

Gardien said, "I remember when Walt Disney's children or relatives came up, they decided that I needed a house, too, so they went up to the woods and found a tree that would be called 'Stretched,' and they made a sign for me, too. They brought it up to me next time they came." Deetjen wanted to pay Ed for the trailblazing, but he said it was his gift to the Inn.

Gardien worked under Deetjen from April 1964, the same year Bill De Groat arrived at the Inn, to July 1969, when he left for Hawaii. Though Ed had his disagreements with Deetjen, he stood in awe of him as well.

> He must have had training in meditation and Yoga. He was a man that had a powerful presence. He could read your mind. Deetjen was in a very high state of spiritual consciousness. He might have even experienced cosmic consciousness. He didn't have to say I believe this or that. He was a Ngor. I felt it an honor to have worked with him. I always considered Grandpa my spiritual father.

When Ed was on his way back from Japan with Kuniyo, his bride-to-be, he received a cablegram that his father had passed away, and when he returned, he learned from Emil White that Deetjen had died at almost the same time. In just under four months after Deetjen's death, Deetjen's Incorporated contacted Ed about becoming manager. He and Kuniyo took over as innkeepers on February 12, 1973, and were married in a Buddhist ceremony in the Enchanted Room, May 12, 1973. They operated the Inn until February 1984, and wrote a 14-page report of some 31 projects completed on their watch.

Between 1964 and 1984, Gardien recalled many in the entertainment industry who visited or stayed at the Inn: John Denver, Robert Redford, Clint Eastwood, Steve Allen, Kim Novak, Joan Collins, Dyan Cannon, Kathryn Grayson, Judy Collins, Mia Farrow, Peter Sellers, Sharon Tate, Sue Lyon, Tuesday Weld, Ena Hartmann, Joan Baez, and Jeff Bridges, who got Gardien a walk-on part in *The Jagged Edge*.

FACING: Stokes Evans, Deetjen's talented handyman making shelves in the workshop that is now a rental named in his honor "Stokes."

LEFT: Sculptor Jim Hunolt worked only one summer for Deetjen. He was on his way around the world but stayed instead at the Inn's Top House. He became an apprentice to Jeffers' and Deetjen's friend, sculptor Gordon Newell. Hunolt works in Big Sur and Darwin, California, showing his work locally at the Coast Gallery. Hunolt had help from fellow Darwin/Big Sur resident Hal Newell, Gordon's son, and Pierre when mounting his *Unicorn Shadow* for display. Of the relationship between Hal's father, Gordon Newell, and Deetjen, Hal says, "They drank and recited poetry!"

Friends of the Inn   137

"John Denver," Ed remembered, "was a very, very tender man, and he brought his children to the Inn. Once we had tied a rope to one of the trees and we were swinging across the canyon, and Denver was swinging with his children."

Though "Sur" means "south" in Spanish, Gardien learned that it meant "divine melody" in Sanskrit. He began giving small brass bells to guests, friends, and even an occasional pet. With the bell, he offered the following words: "Let the Divine Melody enter into your very being and keep this bell as a symbol of all the things you value most in your love of life."

MORE THAN STORIES . . .

Everyone thinks that everyone else has a better memory of those times. One person says to ask another. Soon one realizes the multitude of pebbles that blend and belong in the aggregate used to pour and form a foundation.

Rita Gatti, a fine woodworker, singer, and guitarist, recalls "all the cats and dogs that were there when Helmuth was alive," and that after Deetjen was asleep, "we would play music [folk songs] into the wee hours. Bob DeFord would play washtub base. I remember once Pete Seeger's brother John and his bride, Judith, came on their honeymoon. We had a lot of fun with them . . . singing. . . . All those copper pots . . . were banged on with wooden spoons during those music hours. . . . I remember us all walking down the middle of the road . . . no cars . . . spending all night there at the [Esalen] baths."

Mimi Anderson Fain said, "I had literally left my family home at the age of 18 and walked right into the heart of the Inn and Deetjen and Big Sur, and they into mine. Not to mention the heart friends that I encountered during that time there. . . . No matter that there is not lots of communication that goes on over the years—we are connected by hearts." . . .

More than stories, I remember the turn of head, facial expressions, the cigarette in his mouth with one eye closed, and the smoke curling up around his face—his laugh, his anger, his guttural "Gawhhhhh," his quietness, his smile, his calling for "Edit" [Edith] or "Bawb" [Bob] or calling for the dogs by name, the twinkle in his eye with all that wisdom in there. Certain residents of Big Sur (or strangers) would come through the door and sit at the bar. He would look at them, and then walk away and comment, "No scruples." (Was that wisdom gained through long years of living, or ESP? I am not sure, but I paid attention when he said those things). . . . It was so hard to be away from there—to go away from there. . . . So many good things were formed in me there. It was a place where a true education could take place. . . . Such a great blessing for the world and all who have been there and still come, and are just now discovering it.

One frightening but poignant memory, Mimi recalled, occurred on a blustery evening when she stayed in Top Piano, "the wonderful middle room with the big

ABOVE: Martin "Hubbs" Hubback (shown with Snowy), the maintenance manager, oversees the basic operation of the Inn's infrastructure. Hubbs is a valued member of the Big Sur Volunteer Fire Brigade. FACING: Tara Nutter and Faye Harrington on the buckboard wagon seat outside Grandpa's Room.

windows that slid open and also went out to a deck." . . .

> I thought I heard a sound coming from a distance, but the wind was blowing and it was raining. I felt something was amiss, but what could it be? I listened and again it sounded, and now it sounded like a voice calling from a distance. I jumped up, opened the window, and listened. I heard it again. It was Grandpa hollering at the top of his lungs, "Mimiiiiiii, Miiiiiiiimiiiiiiiii!" He was calling for help and I did not know how long he had been calling. When I got there, he was not there, not in his bed. I called "Grandpa, Grandpa, where are you?" Then I looked in the last, most impossible place, his bathroom, that tiny-little-smaller-than-the-smallest-closet toilet room. He had fallen, and was wedged. . . . I did not know how long he had been there . . . but by God he called and I heard him through the wind, the rain, the closed doors and windows, all of it!

A CHILD'S-EYE VIEW

"I remember when we started coming to the Inn. I was seven," said, Richard Levine, who came with his parents Wally and Ilene. He enjoyed a special relationship with Deetjen.

> When Grandpa realized I was old enough to work, instead of just hang out and be a kid, he'd take me into town, and no matter how long or short my hair was, he'd want to take me to the Pine Inn where there was this old barber shop, and get my hair cut. I was about 16 by then. We'd do some town runs, and get dropped off at The Bistro [in Carmel] and he'd order me a liverwurst sandwich. He'd always have liverwurst on rye and a can of Coors beer. He'd order for me. "He's not old enough," the waiter would

ABOVE: Tracy Brockway with Sadie in Castro Canyon. Tracy remained in Big Sur since working for Grandpa in the '60s and recently returned to the Inn after many years. She has given many hours of service to the Big Sur Volunteer Fire Brigade.

Brockway recalls not having to work on her birthday, even though she'd just arrived a month before. She has vivid memories of Edy, who hired her. "On Saturday night, she would always dress up in those beautiful silk and velvet and satin gowns, with jewels and lipstick and rouge and eye shadow—with her cigarette holder . . . She'd have an Old Fashioned and sit on the little stool in the kitchen and ask Bill to cook her some okra. When Mr. Deetjen went to bed, she'd sit at the head of the Family Table and do the books. The minute he went out the door, she'd say, 'All right, put on Donovan!'"

say. A couple of times he slammed his cane on the table and said, "Bring him what I'm having!" Then we'd go over the hill to do the rest of the errands. Levine remembers that his mom, who never worked for Deetjen, was part of the volunteer army. It was just a love people had of the place that would make them want to contribute in various ways.

She would just help out, wait tables or wash dishes or make coffee.

Making that coffee—you had to stir it with your pinky out! And you couldn't scrape the sides or the cone. One night Grandpa and my dad drank so much Paisano we took him home in a wheelbarrow.

There was a patch of pavement about 15 feet long by 2 feet wide outside the Hayloft. As he approached on the walk home at night, Deetjen would say, "We're coming to the freeway."

You had to be sure all the candles were lit. You had to be very aware. That covered everything. I remember when the Molera Fire came, he said maybe he wouldn't have to take me to the barber shop. I had long hair, and Grandpa said maybe the fire would burn it off! He turned me on to Benjamin Franklin's Glass Harmonica, and a lot people still don't know what that is. I remember when he played Julian Bream.

TO HEAL MY SOUL

The following memory gives us a different view, an Old World perspective, of Deetjen as he related to European guest George Keeleric. He wrote the recollection on January 30, 1979:

My first visit to Big Sur Inn was in 1960. I had a business appointment in Los Angeles at lunch time, and had decided to drive down from Berkeley along the Coastal Highway, necessitating the—for me—ungodly departure hour of five in the morning. I did not reach Los Angeles. After passing Hurricane Point, I was feeling so drowsy that I could not keep my eyes open, and when I passed Deetjen's Big Sur Inn, I decided to stop for a few hours to catch a couple of hours sleep. I stayed four days.

In the next couple of years, whenever I felt I had to heal my soul, I went down to the Inn to stay a few days, and thus was the beginning of my friendship with Deetjen.

We had something in common, of course, both being Europeans, he from Norway, I from Denmark, and we could easily agree on our respective country's superiority over all others—starting with the Swedes. On most other subjects, we completely disagreed.

My years of 1962–64 were spent abroad, but when I got back, I decided to live in Big Sur and rented a small cottage at Rogers 3-Acres. When I first entered Deetjen's Inn, I did not think he would recognize me after the years of absence; also, I pretended never to have been there before. Half-way through my meal, however, he turned around and said: "How were things in Denmark?" His memory was fantastic.

In spite of our continual mutual leg-pulling, between us it was always "Mr." Deetjen and "Mr." Keeleric, as is customary between Europeans of our vintage. When we dined together at his table beside the bar, our discussions ranged over a vast area.

ABOVE: Assistant Manager Doris Jolicoeur is "a Canadian from Vermont," she says.

His favorite subject, however, was metaphysics, and I being an agnostic and skeptic, gave him all the opportunities to exercise his Guru tendencies. Once the discussion turned to palmistry, and I did the obligatory scoffing. I told him, however, that I could do something with my thumb, which few could do, namely, bend it backwards ninety degrees. Deetjen did not say anything, but removed his hand from his blue denim trousers, lifted his hand and bent his thumb backwards ninety-one degrees. Then he called one of his "slave-disciples," and sent him to his room to fetch a book. The book turned out to be on palmistry. He opened it on the chapter, "The Thumb" and let me read it. I am not going to incriminate myself (or Deetjen) about what it said of our personalities. Deetjen offered me the loan of the book for further study, which I refused. I was not going to have my disbelief shaken.

I left Big Sur for Ireland because I had too much leisure on my hands. If Stokes' job had fallen vacant at that time, I might well have renounced the world and joined the other refugees from the United States, such as Dick Hartford, Charlie Levitsky, and Paula of TWA.

FOR REVELATION

Employees who worked for both Helen and Helmuth had an entirely different experience from those who knew Grandpa as solo innkeeper. In 1957, when Alan Pappe worked for the Deetjens, Big Sur had nowhere near the traffic of today. Whatever notoriety it had in those days mainly had to do with Henry Miller, whose girlfriend, Caryl Hill, worked at the Inn for a time, and lived at the Top House. A sign at either end of the highway warned visitors that the road was not patrolled at night. Indeed, many times one could drive to Big

Sur in those days and never see another car—in either direction. Quite a contrast from today's bustling pace. Pappe gives a taste of the days when "Deetjen and Grandma Deetjen were alive and well."

I used to shop in Carmel and Monterey 3 times a week with Grandma, always an interesting experience. Grandma always sampled the Bakery Goods. I used to get on her case about this, but she was the boss. . . . She was always up early, knew everything that was going on, watching from her window. . . . She was a very bright lady—very sharp. Deetjen on the other hand was a man of very few words—sometimes no words, just a shake of the head if you were doing something he disapproved of. I used to play jazz piano in the dining room, and he always would shake his head "no," but I ignored it and played anyway.

I remember a small sign on the wall that said, "You must learn to do the things that must be done." I've quoted this since 1957. There was another very small sign that said, "1 + 1 = 1"!

Deetjen used to love his red wine. Grandma would always ask me who the wine was for (but she knew). I told her: You get the bakery goodies—Deetjen gets a little wine. He told me he drank for "REVELATION." People said he was a drunk, but there's no truth in this, not an ounce. There's a very special vibe here, if you walk around quietly, you can feel it.

ABOVE: Bruce Neeb brings his talent, cordiality, and management background to the current operation of the Big Sur Inn Preservation Foundation.
BELOW, RIGHT: Edith O'Ryan and Deetjen's staff, c.1964

FIFTIETH ANNIVERSARY

Betty Sue Walters first came to Deetjen's in 1972. Though she was away from the Inn for a time, she remains the only person currently employed who was on the payroll when Deetjen died. She knows the Inn and the area thoroughly, and over time has collected a variety of invaluable information on the Inn. Honeymooners wrote this touching

recollection to her at the Inn. Hard to imagine for today's Highway One travelers, but the businesses once closed in winter (as did the road—and from time to time, it still does). While businesses enjoy a seasonal spike in spring and summer, no one now would consider business on the coast as seasonal. They remain open year round; not the case in the following account, a letter to Bettie Sue from Joan and Bill Smith.

January 23, 2001

When I talked with you on the phone, I told you briefly about our first visit to Deetjen's on Christmas night 1951, when there was a room at the Inn for two strangers! We were on our "Honeymoon Trip" headed for Pacific Grove, when about dark, a storm blew in near Lucia. We started looking for a place to stop and eat, and the first place we came to was Deetjen's.

We could see a glimmer of light inside, and as Bill got out of the car, a man in a yellow rain slicker and lantern approached. He said the restaurant was closed in the winter. But after hearing of our situation, he thought he could take care of us, and invited us to come in.

He sat us down at a small table in a side room by a beautiful fire. Then he lit a candle and poured two water tumblers of red wine and told us he'd be back shortly. When he returned, he said that he and his wife were about to have their Christmas dinner, and would like to share it with us!

We were overwhelmed and very touched by their kindness to us. Deetjen returned with a covered tray and a most memorable Christmas dinner—Roast pork, browned potatoes, onions, carrots, and cranberries. With the wine, candlelight, warm fire, and the storm, it was all quite wonderful and very romantic. The memory has warmed our hearts all these many years.

After dinner, Deetjen returned, and the three of us sat by the fire and talked. Oh, how enjoyable that was! At that time, there were rooms upstairs, and that's where we spent the night, with the wind and rain beating against the window.

Thru the years, we have been back many times with family and friends. We look forward to once again sitting by that same fireplace and having dinner, and remembering that special time 50 years ago.

Sincerely
Joan and Bill Smith

The Deetjens journey from privilege to penury to self-made security. The couple who sought seclusion, an exiled pair, ended by offering an open invitation to humanity. Had they known the trials that lay ahead, they would have doubtless chosen the same campsite at the end of the trail, and waited there for the world to find them. As Whitman wrote in *The Song of the Redwood-Tree*, "Here build your homes for good . . . ." They more than met his challenge.

ABOVE: Ed Gardien managed Deetjen's on two separate occasions and made substantial improvements to the Inn. He added Norwegian wood-burning stoves to rooms that had never had heat and paved the drive and parking areas that were once dusty in summer and muddy in winter.
BELOW: Peggy Thestrup with Lama. Peggy worked for the Inn at the time of Deetjen's death.

Friends of the Inn

INSCRIPTION FOR A GRAVESTONE

I am not dead, I have only become inhuman:
That is to say,
Undressed myself of laughable prides and infirmities,
But not as a man
Undresses to creep into bed, but like an athlete
Stripping for the race.
The delicate ravel of nerves that made me a measurer
Of certain fictions
Called good and evil; that made me contract with pain
And expand with pleasure;
Fussily adjusted like a little electroscope:
That's gone, it is true;
(I never miss it; if the universe does,
How easily replaced!)
But all the rest is heightened, widened, set free.
I admired the beauty
While I was human, now I am part of the beauty.
I wander in the air,
Being mostly gas and water, and flow in the ocean;
Touch you and Asia
At the same moment; have a hand in the sunrises
And the glow of this grass.
I left the light precipitate of ashes to earth
For a love-token.

Coast live oak and Calfornina bay laurel. Photo by Kodiak Greenwood.

Yellow Lupine and Mountains. Photo by Kodiak Greenwood.

eight

CONTRAST

The world has many seas, Mediterranean, Atlantic, but here is the shore
of the one ocean.
And here the heavy future hangs like a cloud; the enormous scene; the
enormous games preparing
Weigh on the water and strain the rock; the stage is here, the play is
conceived; the players are not found.

I saw on the Sierras, up the Kaweah Valley above the Moro rock, the
mountain redwoods
Like red towers on the slopes of snow; about their bases grew a bushery of
Christmas green,
Firs and pines to be monuments for pilgrimage
In Europe; I remembered the Swiss forests, the dark robes of Pilatus, no
trunk like these there;
But these are underwood; they are only a shrubbery about the boles of the
trees.

      Our people are clever and masterful;
They have powers in the mass, they accomplish marvels. It is possible Time
will make them before it annuls them, but at present
There is not one memorable person, there is not one mind to stand with
the trees, one life with the mountains.

Keeping the Inn

What Deetjen built was like home—only better. With his wife, Helmuth Deetjen crafted a home that honors the land itself—a tall order in Big Sur. With simplicity, love, and modest means, he matched the land's timeless beauty and serenity. The canyon that was their home became a surrogate home to travelers worldwide—travelers weary of cities, weary of sameness—all in search of tranquility.

"People, they come and go, most of them. Very few stay—for good. I think they are looking for something they can't find where they came from, something they are missing in the big cities," Deetjen remarked in Bob Blaisdell's film, *Big Sur: The Way It Was*. The look and feel of the Big Sur Inn suggests a life the world longs for but has forgotten how to build and how to inhabit. Perhaps today, more than when Deetjen observed that longing, people need a place like the Inn. It provides a transitory shelter for visitors. The authenticity within its walls is something that one can examine. Just as Deetjen gave Zen-like attention to every detail, visitors can find features about the Inn that evoke a sense of well-being. Just as carefully executed feng shui design may create a feeling of uncomplicated comfort, similarly Deetjen's creates a deep sense of peace with its casual mix of simple knick-knacks and genuine antiques.

To keep the timelessness of the Inn, to keep it a place that resonates with the mountains, the redwoods, and the near migratory patterns of people, requires intense devotion. Big Sur Inn has a dedicated staff, and over the years, though change has been inevitable, the feeling most have is that the changes have made the Inn better in nearly every instance. It has taken the efforts of workers, managers, volunteers, and the visitors themselves to

FACING: Hearth in the Restaurant Fireplace Room, Christmas 1966. Courtesy of Elizabeth Martin and the late Carmel Martin Jr.
TOP: Beginning of the Inn—Deetjen stands with his first mailbox in 1938 before building got underway in earnest. His vision first involved a pick and shovel. His first building, the mailbox, demonstrates Deetjen's woodworking skills.
ABOVE: The labor of his lifetime firmly in the past, Deetjen collects his mail in 1972, just a few months before he passed away, leaving the challenge to a select few creative, dedicated people.

RIGHT: The ongoing operation required the expertise of people who not only loved Big Sur Inn and had Deetjen's interest at heart, but who could brainstorm, troubleshoot, and come up with an action plan that would protect and enhance the Inn, repair potential code violations, and yet not disturb the very warmth and ambiance visitors cherished. Kent Seavey, Carmel "Cappy" Martin Jr., and Don McQueen formed just the trio of talent necessary for the mission. They presided over this 1990 ceremony placing Deetjen's on the National Registry of Historic Places.
BELOW: Coventry's back cover of Kent Seavey's 1992 *Big Sur Inn: A Brief History* shows the Fireplace Room of the restaurant.

sustain the ageless nature of Deetjen's. To this end, a few caring, creative souls stepped forward to meet the challenges of overseeing the Inn.

THE INN FOUNDATIONS

Just as building the Inn required a solid foundation, the Inn also required strong support once the Deetjens passed away. Credit for creating the vision that allowed the Inn to survive goes to the late Carmel Martin Jr. (Deetjen's attorney), to Kent Seavey, and to Don McQueen.

Cappy, as friends of Carmel Martin Jr. knew him, loved Big Sur Inn, and knew the coast throughout his life. Martin's widow, Elizabeth Martin, recalled that not long after she married Cappy, Deetjen passed away. The couple drove down the coast for the service. "I remember that so vividly, walking up that path, and I can remember the tree where we stopped. We all carried a rose. I thought, 'This is so lovely!'"

"When it had to do with clients, we didn't discuss things. He was old school," Mrs. Martin recalled, but about Cappy's dedication to the Inn and to Deetjen, she said, "I think it reminded him so much of the times when he went down the coast with his father. They used to walk the trails and go fishing."

Whatever the reason for his abiding interest in maintaining the Inn, it was clearly a labor of love. The other board members—Kent Seavey, Don McQueen, and newer members Jonathan McQueen and Roger Buckout—are intent in overseeing the Inn, to monitor but not to micro-manage. Their involvement remains somewhat on the order of Grandpa's "Three A's:" Alertness, Awareness, Attention!

THEN AND NOW

Long-time Deejten's, Inc., board member Kent Seavey wants the Inn to be "a clean, well-operated place that does the same thing it did for Deetjen. We have a particular clientele that tends to like a more rustic environment.... It's our mandate to maintain it as historically correct as we can. Whatever form it has, as time goes by, places like the Chateau Fiasco [1962] when they hit their 50-year mark, will become part of the Historic Inn."

Seavey guided the group through the application process for having the Inn placed on the National Register of Historic Places. Michal Moore, Monterey County supervisor at the time, knew Martin, and got to know Kent Seavey when Moore was the chairman of the county parks commission. He brought Seavey to Big Sur Inn when the County of Monterey was considering operating the Inn, before the formation of Deetjen's, Inc.—the nonprofit foundation that oversees the Deetjen's Big Sur Inn Preservation Foundation, which became the management arm of the twin organizations. Moore worked for Deetjen a brief time. He liked to write poetry and held a place in his heart for the Inn, according to Seavey, who is the historical coordinator for the Inn.

"I just gave them guidance and advice," he said. When Monterey County reversed its original decision to operate the Inn, Seavey suggested it could continue to operate as an Inn, noting that it was basically intact as it was constructed. "Why don't we put it in the National Register so it's a nonprofit, and then we can pour all the money back into the Inn," Seavey recommended. Martin and the board agreed, and Seavey wrote the National Register nomination. In so doing, the board built a commendable model that continues to serve Deejten's, its staff, local residents, and international travelers.

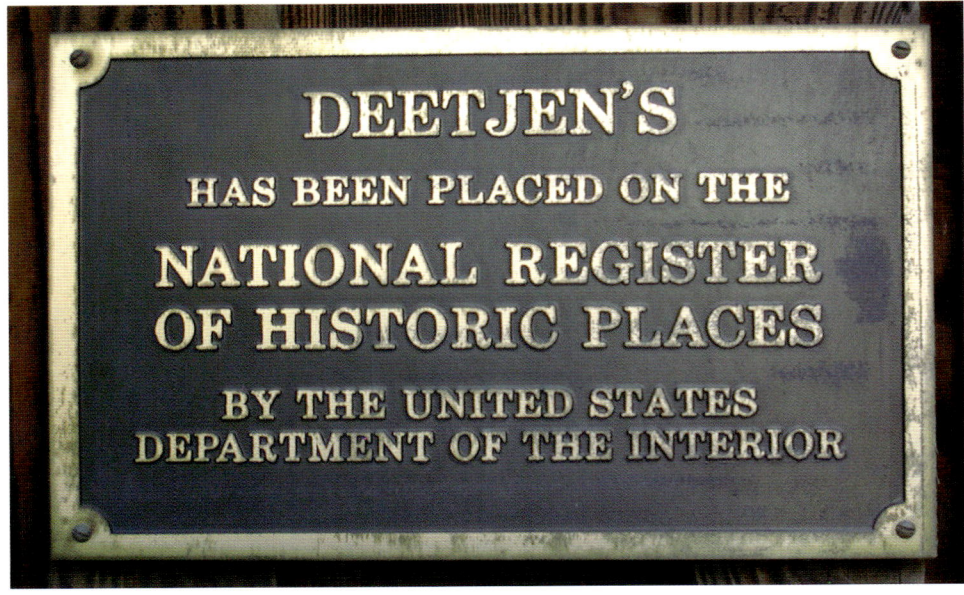

ABOVE, TOP: In 1965 the Van Gogh Room, clean and a bit worse for wear, attracted loyal guests.
LEFT: The Van Gogh Room now has new luster and cheer without any loss of Deetjen's character that attracts return visitors. The Inn hired Clovis Harrod to upgrade the rooms. She began with comfortable mattresses and then new spreads and curtains, saying, "If I do my job the way I see it, my work will be invisible."
LEFT: The plaque from the Department of the Interior hangs just outside the side door to the restaurant.

Keeping the Inn

ABOVE: Keeping the Inn's beauty and rusticity intact as close as possible to Deetjen's wishes would take years to achieve.

BELOW: The current board of Deetjen's Inc.—the 501(c)(3) tax exempt organization overseeing the Inn since Deetjen's death—shown at a 2006 board meeting. From left to right: Roger Buckout, Don McQueen, Jonathan McQueen, Kent Seavey (historian for Deetjen's, Inc.), and Gerald B. Dalton, sitting in for the late Carmel Martin Jr.

FROM THE BOARD

DEETJEN'S, INC.
490 Calle Principal, Monterey, California 93940 Tel: (408) 375-3151

Deetjen's Big Sur Inn is listed on the National Register of Historic Places, and owned by a California educational non-profit corporation called Deetjen's, Inc. Deetjen's, Inc. was established to maintain the Deetjen's Big Sur Inn and property as closely as possible to its original form, while continuing to provide services to visitors, in the style of Mr. and Mrs. Deetjen. It is comprised of a small group of local volunteers who have known and appreciated Deetjen's for many years, and who want to help it retain its unique qualities. Our mission is to enable Deetjen's to continue serving visitors as it always has, while meeting modern health and safety regulations.

Helmuth Deetjen constructed the Inn prior to World War II, in the vernacular wooden building tradition of his native Norway. Its rustic architecture was intended to integrate the Inn into its natural setting of coastal chaparral and the redwoods along Castro Creek. Deetjen's was one of the first visitor facilities offering overnight lodging and meals to travelers along the Big Sur coast, in response to the opening of the Carmel-San Simeon Highway.

Deetjen's has survived relatively unchanged within the ever-more-popular destination of Big Sur. As local businesses adapt to meet the desires of modern travelers, Deetjen's stands firm in its old ways, providing a place for visitors to go back in time, to experience life in Big Sur as it was when Helen and Helmuth Deetjen welcomed travelers into their Inn, many decades ago. With support from the community and from visitors, we will be able to keep Deetjen's as it was, for many generations to come.

Deetjen's, Inc.

Board of Directors

THE PAST IN TOUCH WITH THE FUTURE

Don McQueen is one of Big Sur's larger than life figures. His business experience in the community includes owning and operating a local campground and founding and managing Torre Engineering. Because Don McQueen worked alongside Helmuth Deetjen on many projects, and because he knew Mrs. Deetjen, his interest in maintaining the Inn's history has personal meaning and involves personal experiences. As mentioned, from age 11, McQueen worked with Deetjen on the restaurant, the house that became Henry Miller's, on the original wiring at the Inn, and on laying pipe to the Top House

LEFT: Still cheerful and bright forty years later, the room has the longer lasting warmth of a wood stove, and the delight of guest journals.
ABOVE: Also in the Hayloft building, the Fireplace Room had a distinct 1965 lived-in look.
BELOW: Martin "Hubbs" Hubboack sees small ways to embed Deetjen's Norwegian heritage in the wall of a renovated structure.

and Goat House, both of which are currently in use as staff housing. Therefore, his many memories span several decades. They include a remembrance of Mrs. Deetjen letting the dogs clean their lunch dishes in the early days when he and his brother Glenn worked at the Top House. "After that, Glenn brought his own lunch," McQueen quipped.

McQueen's most indelible Deetjen memory was of a far more serious nature. On December 23, 1941, the Los Angeles–based U.S. tanker *Montebello*, bound for Vancouver, British Columbia, was torpedoed by a Japanese submarine off Piedras Blancas on the southern Big Sur coast. Other shelling would take place along the West Coast during the WWII years, so citizen reports were important. Nepenthe Restaurant hadn't been built yet, but the original log house was there. The only telephone in Big Sur at that point was at the Highway Maintenance Station. McQueen vividly recalled this scene:

> Helmuth Deetjen came running in about 4 o'clock in the afternoon. He told my dad, and I remember him telling him in very broken English, that he'd been running the whole way, and that there was a Japanese submarine down in the cove between [what's now] Nepenthe and Castro Ranch. He had been walking and saw it and ran all the way down there to get my dad, and my dad called the Army and the Navy. The Navy said they would dispatch torpedo bombers from Palo Alto from those big hangers, and the Army was going to investigate, too.
>
> My dad got in the car with Helmuth Deetjen and I with him, and we went there. We had to walk around the side of the hill where the Phoenix is now, and we looked down there, and sure enough, there they were. The submarine was right inside that little cove, and they were refueling it. It turned out that some of the Japanese fishermen

Keeping the Inn   153

in Monterey had put tanks in many coves up and down the coast and filled them with fuel over time, and the Japanese could go in there and get fuel. Sure enough, that's what they were doing. We were sitting there very quietly, watching, when suddenly an Army lieutenant and two guys showed up. They had a machine gun on a palette and they carried it out there and set it up and started shooting. And I never will forget seeing them just run, and with an ax, chop the hose, and two minutes later, they were gone. He was shooting at them all the time, but he never hurt anything at all. Within five minutes, the torpedo bombers came over, but it was already gone.

During this same period, dogs and officers on horseback patrolled the coast along the Monterey Peninsula, from Carmel, Pebble Beach, Pacific Grove, along the shores to Monterey, and to Fort Ord. Shops were darkened and black-out shades were required for houses, but the Big Sur coast was harder to patrol.

McQueen's historical perspective and professional experience as an engineer and heavy machinery operator lends expertise to the Deetjen's board.

Jonathan McQueen was born and raised on the Big Sur coast and worked for his father, Don, at Torre Engineering. He holds a degree in mechanical engineering from the University of California at Davis, and an MA in business administration from Columbia University. McQueen has worked for a computer firm in San Diego, but he brings local experience to the Deejten's board.

Roger Buckout brings out-of-the-area expertise to the board. His experience in construction management projects will continue to aid the Deejten's, Inc. board. Buckout is the board's newest member, following the death of Carmel Martin Jr.

FROM GRANDPA'S WILL: THE LEGACY LIVES ON

Helmuth Deetjen's will leaves to future generations the "sole and absolute discretion for the purpose of maintaining the Big Sur Inn as a restaurant and Inn for transient guests so that the public may enjoy the natural beauty, charm, and scenery of Big Sur Inn and so that the Big Sur Inn be maintained in nearly the same manner and style as operated by the Deetjens during their lifetime."

To all those who dedicate themselves to keeping Big Sur Inn as his will requests—"as a restaurant and inn for transient guests so that the public may enjoy the natural beauty, charm and scenery of the Big Sur Inn . . . in nearly the same manner and style as practicable, as maintained by me at the date of my death"—we remain forever in your debt.

BELOW: The Jeffers Corner of the restaurant in 1974, was an inviting area.
BELOW, BOTTOM: The Jeffers corner of today holds a bit more history, but maintains the Inn's charm.

FROM THE MANAGEMENT

Deetjen's Big Sur Inn
Preservation Foundation

Deetjen's, an awkward collection of 'untouched' remarkably charming structures, remains one of the last authentic representatives of a commercial nature in Big Sur, dating back to the thirties. All other establishments on the coast seem to have been bought out, faded away, burned in fires, marginalized, or modernized in physically noticeable ways.

Deetjen's is more than simply a collection of buildings, historic or not that we rent to commercially operate as The Inn. It is more than a rustic period piece to amuse or delight the senses. It is an artful, if rustic, carefully controlled physical setting, always changing and forever, in memory at least, the same. The Inn is an evocative ambiance or sensibility, if you will, more akin to a nostalgic myth. It is this myth we, the staff, are here to support. We support this myth by encouraging an attitude that emphasizes authentic, respectful, individualistic, friendly, if at times spicy, homegrown, and neighborly contact with our guests. In this setting and with the authentic service we endeavor to provide, our guests are offered a personal glimpse of a tangible and perhaps remembered yearning for a simpler more gracious, personally honest and definitely quieter, less stressful times, the past.

Our role as current staff members is to protect, maintain and enhance the nostalgic myth this setting evokes, today and into a future that may well include none of us. This is our goal. A pleasurable and worthy mandate it is indeed.

Bruce Neeb

General Manger
Deetjen's Big Sur Inn

ABOVE, TOP: Overseeing the Inn in this Brook Elgie photo, Grandpa Deetjen, his characteristic unlit cigarette in place, keeps an eye toward the future while staying in touch with the past.
ABOVE: In March, the well-cared-for gardens at the Inn begin a season of profuse flowering that continues into late fall, thanks to Odile Segal and other dedicated gardeners.

Anyone interested in contributing to the ongoing stewardship of this irreplaceable cultural resource is welcome to contact the Board of Directors, Deejten's, Inc., at 490 Calle Principal, Monterey, CA 93940, USA.

THE TREASURE

Mountains, a moment's earth-waves rising and hollowing; the earth too's
 an ephemerid; the stars—
Short-lived as grass the stars quicken in the nebula and dry in their
 summer, they spiral
Blind up space, scattered black seeds of a future; nothing lives long, the
 whole sky's
Recurrences tick the seconds of the hours of the ages of the gulf before
 birth, and the gulf
After death is like dated: to labor eighty years in a notch of eternity is
 nothing too tiresome,
Enormous repose after, enormous repose before, the flash of activity.
Surely you never have dreamed the incredible depths were prologue and
 epilogue merely
To the surface play in the sun, the instant of life, what is called life? I fancy
That silence is the thing, this noise a found word for it; interjection, a jump
 of the breath at that silence;
Stars burn, grass grows, men breathe: as a man finding treasure says "Ah!"
 but the treasure's the essence;
Before the man spoke it was there, and after he has spoken he gathers it,
 inexhaustible treasure.

Mist over Tide Pool, Lobos Rocks in background. Photo by Kodiak Greenwood.

Acknowledgments

Poems by Robinson Jeffers

"Juan Higera Creek" (p. 12), "Credo" (p. 36), Autumn Evening" (p. 39), "On the Cliff" (p. 58), "The House-Dog's Grave" (p. 61), "Divinely Superfluous Beauty" (p. 80), "Hands" (p. 83), "October Evening" (p. 107), "November Surf" (p. 126), "Sign-Post" (p. 129), "Inscription for a Gravestone" (p. 144), "Contrast" (p. 146), and "The Treasure" (p. 156).

The Collected Poetry of Robinson Jeffers, edited by Tim Hunt (c) 1938; renewed 1966 Donnan and Garth Jeffers; (c) by The Jeffers Literary Properties. All rights reserved. Used with permission of Stanford University Press, www.sup.org.

"Carmel Point," (c) 1954 by Robinson Jeffers (p. 15), "Return," (c) 1935, renewed 1963 by Donnan Jeffers and Garth Jeffers (p. 3), "Tor House," (c) 1928, renewed 1956 by Robinson Jeffers (p. 104), from *Selected Poetry of Robinson Jeffers* by Robinson Jeffers. Used by permission of Random House, Inc.

With sincere appreciation to the Robinson Jeffers Tor House foundation for the December 1915 letter to Dr. Lyman Stookey.

Poetry
Robinson Jeffers
Stephen John Kalinich
Peter Melchior
Walt Whitman

Artwork
Jane Chanteau
Robin Coventry
Arch Garner
"Shag" O' Rourke
Charles Pundsack

Photography
Anita Alan
Brooke Elgie
Kodiak Greenwood
Louis Josselyn
Cato Kolaas
Jane Sanders
David Spence
Noel Douglas Walling
Brett Weston

(Photographer Kodiak Greenwood, a native of Big Sur, has absorbed the beauty of the coast and the Santa Lucia Mountains since birth. His vision of nature parallels the photographic giants of Central California. His portraiture and architecture renderings place humanity compassionately in the landscape. View more of his work at kodiakgreenwood.com.)

Endpapers by "Shag" O'Rourke, courtesy of Elizabeth Martin and the late Carmel Martin Jr.

Book/Film
Randall Reinstedt, *Ghosts of the Big Sur Coast*, Ghosttown Production
Robert Blaisdell, *Big Sur: The Way It Was*, Endorphin Productions

Friends of Deetjen's Big Sur Inn

I am grateful to Gibbs Smith and his talented, dedicated staff: Anita Wood, Carrie Westover, Jennifer Maughan, Jennifer Grillone, Katie Newbold, Kurt Wahlner, and Alison Einerson. Special thanks to the Board of Directors for Deetjen's Incorporated: Kent Seavey—Historian, Don McQueen, Jonathan, McQueen, Roger Buckout, and the late Carmel Martin Jr., for their support. To Elizabeth Martin and Marron Martin. To Big Sur Inn and Deetjen's Big Sur Inn Preservation Foundation management, board, and staff: Bruce Neeb, Doris Jolicoeur, Mary Hatch, and Jessica Cichowski. To all those ensnared by the enchantment of the Inn, who stay for years or leave and return. They give Deetjen's its loving character: Bettie Sue Walters, Tracy Brockway, Denise George, Bob Cosgrove, Michael Emmons, Odile Segal, Mary Detrick, Linda and Martin "Hubbs" Hubback, Justin Robarge, Yolanda Rodriguez Perez, Julia Garcia Cortez, and former employee Bill De Groat, who stayed longer at the Inn than anyone except the Deetjens themselves; to Ed and Kuniyo Gardien, who made the Inn a warmer place in so many ways, and to Mimi Anderson Fain who helped, even in France! To Faye Harrington, Rita Gatti, David Morrison, Don Case, Mike and Mary Trotter, Jeanette "Tootie" Trotter, Richard Levine, Kelly Gibbs, Dorcas Fassett Owens, Jean Widaman, Kim Rowe. To Jill Bowers, Jim Wood, Peter King Monk, Peter and Barbara Ind, Ruth Stevens, Jane Chanteau, Ric Villa, Patty Villa, Jan and Dora Kessler, Clovis Harrod, for *invisible work*. Eric Schandall, Peggy Thestrup, John Hodson, Dave Whitney, the Bryne family, Shelley Newell, Leslie Newell, Hal Newell, Jeanne Newell, Abraham Newell, Caryl Hill, Erica Weston, Warren and Helen Leopold, Lu Dodson, Miles Lerner, Henry Benson, and Jack Overholt. Bob Moen, Bill Tashe, and Claire Swick, for clowning for the camera. Most certainly to Robert DeFord, keeper of many memories, and the faith. To my son Noel Douglas Walling, for exactly everything—a clear view and such a camera! Thanks beyond thanks to Lisa Meckel—eloquent poet, extraordinary friend. Special thanks to the Robinson Jeffers Tor House Foundation, its board, staff, and docents: Lindsay Jeffers, Aengus Jeffers, Alex Vardamis, Fran Vardamis, Elliot Ruchowitz-Roberts, Marie Holmes, Ripple and Vince Huth, Mary Aldinger, Carol Dixon, Rob Kafka, James Karman, Robert Brophy, Tim Hunt, Jane Sanders, and Taelen Thomas. To the Robinson Jeffers Association. To Colin E. Kuster, Anne Hagemeyer Morris, Alan Pappe, Joan and Bill Smith. To sculptor Jim Hunolt, for information on the Arch Garner sculpture of Robinson Jeffers and for his lifelong love of the Inn. To Jeff Garner, for detailing the sculpture's origin at Occidental College. To Pat Hathaway, essential photo archivist of California Views, for honoring and preserving the Central Coast past; to Mark Lolik and Jeff Califano of Bay Photo Lab of Monterey; and to Martin Dooley, for opening even when closed. To Ariane De Pree-Rajfez at Stanford University Press; Caryn Burtt and Deborah Foley at Random House, Inc.; Shari Ryan and Elizabeth Oravetz of Liberty-Ellis Foundation, California Historical Society, Carmel Heritage Society, Big Sur

Historical Society; and John P. Byrne, National Register of Historic Places, Norwegian-American Historical Association, Sons of Norway, and the Vesterheim Norwegian-American Museum. To Julie Robertson from the Honeymoon Room. To May Waldroup, in the name of independent booksellers everywhere. To Susan Melchior and Morris Sheppard. To Kodiak Greenwood for contributing to the graphic wholeness of this book. To Brooks Institute of Photography, for recognizing and enhancing the graphic genius of Kodiak Greenwood. To Dr. Richard Bossone, wherever you are. To screen writer/director Hampton Fancher, who inspires without even trying. To the Deetjen Family in Norway, whose native son enriched the lives of American and international travelers (especially to Trond Deetjen and Clara Deetjen); Paul Sandoey, for his translations from Norwegian; to Fran Vardamis (again), for Norwegian translations, Bergen Tourist Information Board: Cato Kolaas for Bergen photographs, Cily Samuelsen, and Jane Saelemeyer, for a link to the past; to Scott Hale at Brett Weston Archive. To Anita Dickhuth, photo archivist, editor, and appraiser, for her German translations and photo advice. To Dennis Copeland and Victor Henry, archivists at Monterey Public Library, and to Denise Sallee, Research Librarian at Harrison Memorial Library in Carmel, Dick Foreman of Foreman Art, David Lees for web design, Terry Glasco at Virtual Silk, Evelyn Starr, Greg Hyde and Star Reirson (from the Lesser Geek). To Jay Fukushima, for patience and numerical assistance and to Alex Cruz for technical expertise. To poets Ric Masten and Patrice Vecchione, for silver dollars and found poems, and to Catherine Wenner, for Tai Chi and the Staffordshire memory. To Jewel Speer (and her dear Bob), for keeping the grace of living alive, and to Mary Jo Morton Cain and John Atkinson for Deetjen Family oil paintings. To Charles Douglas Walling: Smooth sailing, dear man. To Lang, too. To Reed Cripe, Brigga Mosca, Oliver Cripe, and Larry Pahl at *Monterey County Magazine,* and to Darlene Bagwell, Monterey County Recorder's Office. To Al Jardine and family, and to Stephen John Kalinich, for caring, thoughtful contributions. To Michael Caplin, Alan Perlmutter and Nancy Sanders, Dick Costigan, Sam Goldeen, and all who keep the coast's home vigil; to Gary and Emma Koeppel, John Batz, Carol Shadwell, Sally and Frank Packard, Marty and Ted Hartman, Jeff Norman, Shawna Garritson, Sam Goldeen, Eby Wold, Erin Grafill Birmingham, Lygia Chappellet, Magnus Toren, and so many others who keep art and literature alive on the coast. To Jay Marden, Dina Ruiz Eastwod, Pam Gillooly, Ramona Nason, and Kelly Au at UPS—so helpful. To Paul Behan—for believing. To Bill and Luci Post, and the Harlan family. To the children of Captain Cooper School, Big Sur Home School, Apple Pie Preschool, Esalen's Gazebo School, and Pacific Valley School. Carry on the caring traditions. Keep our coast and your lives vibrant. To Carla Ross at Merritt School of Nursing in Oakland, thanks! Also, David Spence of Beachcomber Inn for the aerial photo of Grandpa's Carrot Patch, and to the ever-faithful Ed Culver, who brought mail, sustenance, and news to many a Highway One artist, craftsman, and writer. To Joe McLellan, who learned patience from Deetjen, and to Robert Blaisdell, who practiced it in *Big Sur: The Way It Was* by Endorphin Productions. To Brooke Elgie for forty-year-old photos from the North 40. To Diane Cleary, who made her home a Norwegian student's haven. To Allegro in Carmel, for allowing us to "burn a table" or two. To Michal Moore, too. To Stephanie Leggett and Robert Parco, still the best organizers I know! To Randall Reinsredt and Ghosttown Publications, for his Grandpa tale from *Ghosts of the Big Sur Coast.* To the Central Coast Lighthouse Keepers and Monterey Bay Aquarium, Guide Shift 2B—just the best! To Jeri and Bill Miller, and Raetta Romero, Gloria Mc Millan, Tracy and Dave Griffiths, and Marge Kinney and their families—friends who put me up and put up with me through all these years. To Stuart Wasser and Ellie Boys O'Neill, for a refreshing respite. And Val Hoover: thanks for the genealogical beginnings. To Linda, Travis, and Selena Henderson, for such kindness. Barbara Wagner and Marilee Farrance of Finnegan Watch. All the thanks in the world cannot cover all its people. You know if you have helped me along the jagged rock and smooth dirt pathways of my life, and this work. You will know if you have contributed something to the Inn—an antique dish, a book, a memory in the Inn's shared journals. If you did, your name belongs here: Thanks to you, _____.

In Memory and Deep Appreciation

To the Legacy of Helen and Helmuth Deetjen

Many over the years have contributed to keeping the Inn operating in the manner the Deetjens envisioned, as a refuge for travelers seeking a home away from home. So, to the families of all who, like the Deetjens themselves, loved and maintained the Inn and have passed on, please know how grateful today's visitors are that your loved ones kept that vigil. Among so many, deep appreciation goes to the Deetjens' friend and handyman Stokes Evans and their friend and accountant Edith O'Ryan, both of whom have rooms named for them. To Allen McQueen, Glenn McQueen, Frank Trotter, Walt Trotter, Richard Trotter, Doris Fee, Peter Melchior, Mike Anderson, Gordon Newell, George De Groat, Everett Makowski, Harry Iverson, George Keeleric, Robin Coventry, Emil White, Henry Miller, Harrydick Ross, Bob Greenwood, Barbara Blake, Arch Garner, Bert Acker, Bill Tangeman, Lance Thestrup, and Andy Gagarin.

For Katharine Douglas Sobey Walling, who made the hard times easier. For my mother, Rebecca Daniels, who first drove me along the Carmel–San Simeon Highway, cautioning me repeatedly not to lean so far out the window. And for my father, James Marion Daniel, who would have loved it here.

On a deeply personal note, to the memory of Gary Alan Antoine, without whom this writer would never have called Big Sur home, and to Minnie Humphreys Robertson, beloved Grannie, who was never happier than she was at Deetjen's. Your hands and hearts have reinforced the Inn and this writer.

With unexpected and deep sadness, I add the name of Carmel Martin Jr. to this list. Martin's devotion to his client Helmuth Deetjen—and to the vision of both Helen and Helmuth—sustained the Inn for more than three decades. His kind and forthright handling of the Deetjen estate remains a model of legal integrity. Humble appreciation goes to the family of the late Carmel "Cappy" Martin Jr., with thanks for his legal guidance through all the transitions of the Big Sur Inn and for championing its preservation.

Afterword

I hope I have honored your years here. The Sunday dinners, the candles that you would never let die. The sparkle in your old but never-weary eyes. Your solemn smile as you sang Sarastro's arias. The crackle of embers that punctuated the fierce tenderness of your words. The poetry you built and nailed to the cross of your life, the redwood stanzas, the ring and rhythm of your hammer through the standing trees and falling stream. Your once able hands clutching the manzanita burl of your cane one last time. The unending joy and now silent wisdom you have given. You recited Emerson: "Only so much do I know, as I have lived." To build a place that matches the rhythm of the human heart, that unites the temporal and eternal, was but one aspect of your genius for living. Your loving gift to the land. The gentle but indelible touch you and Helen bequeathed. You must know that a few delicate souls could not have made it through had you not shared your dream with them. The part of the earth you found to live on embraces you still; a burnt redwood hollow cradles your ashes, bestowing gifts to the spring-soft seedlings. The sense of place you created likewise inspires new and old souls to grow and reach for light.